# Robert T. Moran's Guide to
# Doing Business in Europe

# Robert T. Moran's Cultural Guide to Doing Business in Europe

*Introduction by Michael Johnson*

Butterworth – Heinemann Ltd
Linacre House, Jordan Hill, Oxford OX2 8DP

PART OF REED INTERNATIONAL BOOKS

OXFORD  LONDON  BOSTON
MUNICH  NEW DELHI  SINGAPORE  SYDNEY
TOKYO  TORONTO  WELLINGTON

First published 1991

**British Library Cataloguing in Publication Data**
Moran, Robert T.
 Robert T. Moran's cultural guide to doing business in Europe
 I. Title
 382.094

ISBN 0 7506 0093 4

Printed and bound in Great Britain by Billing & Sons Ltd, Worcester

# Contents

This book is dedicated to past, present and future graduate students at the American Graduate School of Management in Glendale, Arizona. Many are true internationalists and multicultural persons. As such, they will make a difference in the world in which we all live.

# Acknowledgements

The writing and publishing of books result from the combined efforts of many people. This book is no exception.

We wish to thank the many persons who assisted in various phases of the research, especially Harold Edwards, Loribeth Jacobs, Caroline M. McClurg and Timothy White.

Over a period of a year, three very talented persons assisted in a significant way, and we wish especially to thank Michael Landry, Stephanie Moeller and Joaquin Samper. They worked hard and their efforts were critical to the publication of this book.

We also wish to thank Judith Soccorsy who worked on the various iterations in important ways.

*Robert T. Moran*
*Michael Johnson*

# Introduction

There just might be some scope for a new branch of 'chaos theory' in the study of European cultures. The differences among Europeans seem to multiply infinitely upon closer and closer inspection – much like a Mandlebrot set in the new science of chaos in nature. Taking the satellite view as a starting point, Europe's north–south cultural divide is instantly apparent – ice in the north, fire in the south. Don't touch me in Sweden, take my arm in Italy, kiss me (kiss my friend!) in Spain.

Moving in closer, the differences among northern Europeans come into focus. The British see food as fuel; the French make it a fine art. The Germans are stiff and formal; the Norwegians are quick to melt into warm friendships. Still closer, within a single country new splits show up: the Walloons in Belgium are relaxed, fun-loving, attuned to life's pleasures; the Flemings are sterner, more earnest fellows. Closer yet, within a city: a Londoner living in the NW8 postal code zone wants nothing to do with an East Ender whose consonants disappear in a gurgle of glottal stops.

Miraculously, the world's most closely packed and varied cultures coexist more or less peacefully in the cramped space of Western Europe. A history of trouble, 'written in blood', as one author titled his overview study a few years ago, seems to have turned into a period of peace. With some geopolitical common sense and good luck, it may last well into the future.

Now European business is engaged in an effort to integrate. Throughout the 1990s, barriers to the free movement of people, goods and capital will be eliminated among the twelve members of the European Community (EC), creating a marketing target of 323 million relatively affluent consumers. European visionaries foresee the process encompassing such political affairs as foreign policy. The French speak of tomorrow's Europe as a single multilingual country.

The biggest barriers will not be economic or political. The real obstacles will be the deep cultural differences – some inborn, some learned at mother's knee. The clashes can be damaging. Accidentally offensive behaviour of a potential foreign partner can raise false alarms, sow mistrust, and quickly kill off alliances that might otherwise have flourished.

Step one is to understand the partner's cultural quirks. The senior German partner in a joint venture might sit in his office and sulk for days, waiting for his new British colleague to come and pay his respects. The

British partner will wonder what is going wrong. The tension between them would never have happened had German concepts of hierarchy been better understood.

Of course cross-cultural communication is a two-way street. Ideally, two international business executives should meet each other half way. But, in practice, it is the visitor, not the host, who must adapt and understand. In other words, if you are selling, the pressure is on you.

Communicating across cultures is a skill that must be developed. Foreigners do not necessarily want you to imitate them. Skilful interaction is a sensitive process of eliminating your offensive gestures while adopting just the right degree of your counterpart's behaviour. Nothing seems odder than a foreigner trying too hard. Some true-life incidents:

- A Filipino lady executive of a leading hotel chain tells her London clients that the new decor at her hotel 'will knock your socks off'.
- An elegant French lady who keeps a smart Paris restaurant dreads the weekly arrival of an American customer who each time hurtles towards her with lips pursed. He has read somewhere that kissing means 'Hello' in French.
- An Italian showing off his newly acquired Russian proficiency greets colleagues in Leningrad with a hearty *Do svidanya* (goodbye).
- A German executive wonders what the laughter is about when he announces to the waitress in a fine London restaurant, 'I'm feeling ad-wencherous. I'll have the wenison'.

For the business executive, deal-maker, negotiator, consultant or salesman, we hope this book provides a valuable compass for unfamiliar territory.

*Michael Johnson*
*Robert T. Moran*

# 1  Austria

## A GATEWAY TO THE EAST

The majesty of Austria's mountainous terrain is beyond dispute, but in practical terms it acts as a divisive factor. The soaring Alps stand in the interior, inspiring poets and troubadors, but on a more down-to-earth level they somehow prevent social and business activity from gravitating to a centre. It is often easier for Austrians to make contact with partners and markets in Germany and Switzerland than in Austria itself. Yet the Austrian people have clung together since World War II because of pride in their culture and a determination not to allow their identity to be submerged as it was in the unification with Germany after 1938.

As East–West tensions lessen in Europe, Austria finds herself a 'gateway country' with close ties in both directions. This advantage causes an identity problem, however, as Austrians wonder whether they are fundamentally Central Europeans or West Europeans. At the official level, the country seeks to become a member of the European Community nations as soon as possible.

In their relations with others, the Austrians are a gracious and polite people who indicate their consideration and respect through the use of distinctive greetings. Many foreigners misinterpret this as a forbidding formality or stiffness; but for an Austrian it is a respectful gesture to greet an acquaintance in public with *Grüss Gott*, meaning 'May God greet you'. Any kind of request, be it for directions, for a room, for the time, or for an item in the store, begins with *Bitte*, meaning 'Please' and of course should be followed with *Danke*, meaning 'thank you'. Be sure to say goodbye, *Aufwiedersehen*, when you leave a room.

The Austrians are well known for their *Gemutlichkeit*, a happy approach to life. In addition, they are curious and express a strong desire to learn. The average Austrian probably will enjoy an informal conversation about current affairs.

When visiting an Austrian home, you should follow the custom of bringing flowers or a small gift for the hostess. It is appropriate to unwrap the flowers before presenting them to the lady of the house; one should always give an odd number of flowers. Red roses should be avoided because they denote romantic affection.

Male guests should stand when the host enters the room and remain standing until he suggests sitting down. A younger man always rises when an older person enters the room. In addition, men should rise when a woman enters the room or when speaking to a woman who is already standing.

At dinner with Austrians, it is considered to be impolite to begin eating before everyone is ready. During meals, hands should be kept above the table. Potatoes, fish and dumplings (knödel) should not be cut with a knife, as it implies that they are not tender enough.

Austrians are devoted to their families and spend most of their spare time at home. The family unit has nurtured each person and has provided emotional security as well as a sense of identity. Although the family unit is highly regarded, it is not the key to social stature, as it might be in many other European countries. In Austria, society is composed of individuals who belong to groups outside the home; each person is evaluated on the basis of efforts and accomplishments, not heredity.

Social rank is based on education and profession. Those in administrative positions in the government, members of parliament, or university professors are considered of high social status. Today a large and distinct middle class is in place, sharing similar occupations and educational attainments.

Education is compulsory for nine years. If one does not advance to university studies, apprenticeships and vocational training can be provided.

For just about every hobby or sport there is a club, as the Austrians delight in club membership.

The official language is High German although in rural areas people may speak their particular dialect. Austrians will usually be pleased when a foreigner attempts to learn to speak their language or dialect. They tend to be patient, helpful and tolerant of mistakes. English is a required subject in the educational system, and thus is widely spoken. Whenever possible, however, business correspondence should be carried out in German.

When making appointments with an Austrian, it is considered courteous to offer to meet your contact wherever he or she wishes. Correspondence plays a prominent role in business. Punctuality ranks high among priorities. If an appointment cannot be kept, it is considered proper to call ahead and cancel. Prompt handling of correspondence, including telexes, cables and facsimiles, is greatly appreciated even if the answer is negative. Changes in delivery times, prices or models should also be quickly noted.

The hard sell is usually counterproductive. Business strategies should be designed with long-term goals rather than immediate sales.

Austrian businessmen dress in traditional, conservative suits for the work environment.

Austrians are generally quiet and orderly in public and expect others to behave in the same manner.

## HISTORY AND GOVERNMENT

The Republic of Austria lies in Central Europe, bordered by Switzerland, Liechtenstein, Germany, Czechoslavakia, Hungary, Italy and Yugoslavia. Two-thirds of the country is composed of mountainous Alpine regions, with the Alps dominating the western and southern provinces. Austria's population is approximately 7.6 million people, with a near zero growth rate.

Austria was formerly the centre of the Austro–Hungarian Empire, which comprised a large portion of Europe. In 1918, the Austro–Hungarian Empire was dissolved and the remaining territory was divided into separate countries, one of which was called the Republic of Austria. Germany annexed Austria from 1938 to 1945 and incorporated it into the Third Reich.

At the Moscow Conference in 1943, the Western Allies and the Soviet Union announced their intention to restore Austria to its status as a free and independent country. In April 1945, both East and West forces liberated the country from Germany.

Similar to Germany, Austria was divided into zones of occupation. Dr Karl Renner, an elderly Socialist statesman, undertook the task of organizing the Austrian government into a functioning unit. General elections were held and a coalition was formed. Under the Austrian State Treaty of 1955, the allied occupying forces withdrew, allowing Austria to gain its full freedom. In addition, the Austrian Parliament passed a law declaring the country's neutrality. Austria has benefited from its neutrality, encouraging other countries to use Vienna as a home for international organizations.

Since World War II, Austria has enjoyed political stability. The electorate is composed of two major political parties, the People's Party and the Socialists, which together attract approximately 90 per cent of the voting population. The Socialist Party derives most of its support from workers and white-collar employees, and the People's Party draws its strength from businesses, lay Catholic groups and from farmers. The PP advocates conservative policies; and privatization of Austria's nationalized industries, internationalization of its economy, EEC membership, addressing environmental problems.

Austria is a Federal Republic divided into nine *Läender* (provinces), each headed by a governor elected by the provincial legislature. Although most of the governmental authority is held at the federal level, the provinces are responsible for local administration and social welfare matters.

Legislative power rests with the Federal Assembly, which is composed of two houses – the National Council (Nationalrat) and the Federal Council (Bundesrat). The National Council possesses virtually all authority and comprises 183 members, who are elected for 4-year terms from the nine *Läender*. The Federal Council consists of 58 members, who are elected by the legislatures of the nine *Läender*. They serve 4-6 year terms.

The Head of State, the President, is elected by popular vote for a 6-year term. The President appoints cabinet members, and convenes and discontinues parliamentary sessions.

Austria has been a Christian country since the days of the Roman Empire, and the past centuries of religious faith have left traces throughout the nation. Cathedrals, wayside shrines, crucifixes at crossroads, monasteries,and convents dot the countryside. Church membership, however, has been decreasing drastically. Since 1974, approximately 20,000 Austrians have officially withdrawn from the Catholic Church each year. About 88 per cent of the population is Roman Catholic, 6 per cent is Protestant and the remainder is either Jewish or without religious affiliation.

Religion in Austria has been tied to political and occupational allegiances. Debate has always surrounded the Church's social and political role in the country. The Church maintained a strong political role in Austria's affairs until World War II, but since the war the Church and clergy members have had no political affiliation.

## ECONOMY

The Austrian government plays a large role in the economy. The government has long-term objectives to achieve a negligible unemployment rate, a steady annual growth rate combined with minimal inflation, and a strong currency. Yet many economic problems persist.

High levels of public spending, along with a large national debt, have contributed to poor growth of gross domestic product. The high federal budget deficit can be attributed to continued subsidies for the state-owned industries and the government's inability to reduce national indebtedness.

The government has traditionally striven for full employment, but current restructuring and reorganization of the state sector calls for a reduction of its labour force. Economists predict only moderate economic growth in the years ahead, insufficient to prevent the unemployment rate from rising further. In addition, the government's plan to limit the federal budget deficit will not permit an expansionary fiscal policy, limiting job creation. The Austrians pay high taxes in return for social welfare programmes that provide family allowances, medical and dental care, housing subsidies, scholarships and retirement funds.

As with many other European countries, the Austrian economy is dependent on foreign trade. Therefore the government actively pursues a vigorous export policy in order to finance such necessary imports as agricultural and petroleum products.

Austria's imports have traditionally exceeded exports. Attempts to correct the situation have been hampered by a limited range of exportable items: raw materials, semi-finished goods and a handful of traditional exports.

The majority of Austria's trade is with European partners – the European Free Trade Association (EFTA) and with Eastern Europe. Germany is Austria's largest trading partner, followed by Switzerland, Italy, and Great Britain.

Although not yet a member (the application process has begun), Austria trades with the European Community (EC), which accounts for about 60 per cent of its exports and two–thirds of its imports.

## BIBLIOGRAPHY

Arndt, Sven W. (ed.), *The Political Economy of Austria*, Vienna: FPS, 1982.

Docekal, Josef (ed.), *Survey of the Austrian Economy: Data, Diagrams, and Tables*. Vienna: Wirtschaftsstudio des Osterteichischen Gesellschafts- und Wirtschaftsmuseum. 1986.

Federal Press Service, *Austria: Facts and Figures*. Vienna: Federal Press Service, 1986.

Federal Press Service, *Austria, Land of Encounter*. Vienna: Federal Press Service, 1985.

Federal Press Service, *Resistance and Persecution in Austria 1938-1945*. Vienna: Federal Press Service, 1988.

Gardos, Harald and Wagner, Manfred, *Some Aspects of Cultural Policies in Austria*. Paris: UNESCO, 1981.

Katzenstein, Peter J., *Corporation and Change: Austria, Switzerland, and the Politics of Industry*. Ithaca, NY: Cornell University Press, 1984.

# 2 Belgium

## EUROPE'S MELTING POT

Belgium generates a surface gentility that is rarely equalled in other European cultures. A beautiful country, the terrain rolls in from coastal plains in the northwest, through undulating countryside in the centre, to the Ardennes mountains in the southeast. The climate is temperate, without extremes. Most importantly, the people have a small-country practicality about them – a receptivity to outside influence. Indeed, Belgium is one of the few melting pots of Europe.

In first encounters with a Belgian business executive one is likely to be impressed by a sense of great courtesy and earnestness. It is a style that will prove lasting throughout the relationship. Belgian business executives tend to take their work seriously. Friendships are highly valued, and once a foreign business contact has reached this stage, full cooperation can usually be counted upon. As in many European cultures, most business associates do not use first names until a firm friendship has been formed.

A Belgian typically puts great effort into both work and leisure. Leisure means family-oriented pursuits – hobbies, sports, travel, books, and the varied diet of television in this multicultural part of Europe.

When at work, the Belgian may put in as much as 10 hours a day, and overtime is not uncommon for the standard labourer. The productivity average for the Belgian worker is among the highest in Europe. New ideas are carefully and intellectually analysed, and working plans are given a great deal of study. The typical Belgian business manager is hardworking and industrious.

The business culture has a number of special features. More business entertaining is conducted in private homes than in many other countries, and if invited to a person's home, one should send flowers before arriving or come with flowers or chocolates. Avoid sending chrysanthemums, as they are associated with funerals, All Souls' Day and All Saints' Day. A guest should address the head of the household first when greeting a family.

Writing in advance to schedule a business appointment is necessary. Avoid appointments on Wednesdays in Brussels and Mondays in Antwerp, for many businessmen are at a buying or selling luncheon with their customers or suppliers on these 'Bourse Days'.

The Belgians shake hands when meeting for the first time and thereafter both upon arrival and departure. A man should wait for a woman to offer her hand when being introduced. Close friends of the opposite sex often greet each other with a kiss on the cheek. If their hands are dirty or occupied, the Belgian will often extend the wrist or elbow to be shaken instead. The handshake should be quick with light pressure, for a firm, pumping handshake is considered unrefined.

Touching another person while conversing is not a common practice in Belgium as it is in many parts of Europe. Also important to the Belgians is good posture when conversing. Pointing, snapping fingers, or putting hands in pockets in the presence of others is considered bad manners. Casualness is often mistaken for rudeness.

The following summary is a list of some do's and don't's:

- Be punctual for your appointment. The Belgian businessman keeps to his schedule. Arriving early is a good practice.
- The Belgian manager is the person who will make decisions. Therefore be direct and get to the point.
- While you discuss business, be honest, be courteous, and firm. The Belgian businessman believes that he can succeed through hard work.
- Business cards are essential in Belgium, and should be printed in French or Dutch depending on the recipient's preference.
- If you want to invite the Belgian business executive away from the office, suggest a meal. Belgians appreciate the ceremony of eating and drinking. Lunch would be an appropriate time to talk about business; dinner is usually reserved for close friends and family members or as a celebration for successfully concluded deals.
- Don't talk about your family or personal matters in a business environment unless you have established a close friendship.
- If you invite the Belgian couple to dinner, don't talk shop.
- Putting one's feet on the table or sitting on the desk or table is prohibited.
- After finishing the meal, do not bring out your toothpick.

Social life in Belgium is rather conventional. Handwritten or printed invitations are generally used for cocktails, dinners and receptions, and Belgian hostesses expect a written reply. A *pour memoire* is a reminder of an invitation one has accepted, and requires no reply.

Acknowledgement in some form, depending on the relationship, is necessary in the case of announcements of births, communications, engagements, weddings and funerals. The response may be a gift, flowers, a telegram, a personal note or a calling card message. Flowers are widely used as a gesture of appreciation for hospitality and may be sent before or after a social event. Belgian chocolates, which are a speciality, make an appropriate gift.

When eating, one should keep both hands visible without resting elbows on the table. Belgians use Continental manners, with the fork in the left hand and the knife in the right. Meal time is intended to be relaxed and leisurely. Regular meals are usually served in courses, and there may be as many as seven. In restaurants, the bill is usually paid at the table, and in most cases it includes a tip.

Although society demands external conformity, Belgians are very individualistic people. Refinement and external conformity are considered the route to full inward freedom. A man's home is his castle; privacy is a guarded right and it should be respected.

First impressions are important. People will judge a newcomer at first sight and will mentally rank him somewhere in the social order according to appearance. It is important to dress appropriately when on business trips and not to be too casual when meeting a business client for the first time.

## HISTORY AND GOVERNMENT

A constitutional monarchy located on the North Sea coast, Belgium is a land of two clearly separated cultures. Just south of Brussels, the nation's capital, a 'language line' exists. In Flanders, or northern Belgium, the official language is Dutch. In Walloon, Belgium's south, French is the official language. In and around Brussels, both languages are widely spoken, and the Walloon and Flemish communities live side by side. The customs and habits of the Flemings and Walloons differ in many ways, for the two people were influenced by two very different histories.

Over the centuries, Belgium has experienced internal strife as well as a constant ebb and flow of alien people and cultures. Consequently, Belgium is one of Europe's true melting pots, with cultural elements of Celtic, Roman, German, French, Dutch, Spanish, and Austrian origins. Approximately 65,000 German-speaking people reside in the east. Additionally, about 900,000 foreigners reside in Belgium, many working for or attracted by the seat of the European Community's administrative Commission. The European Parliament is expected to move eventually from Strasbourg to Brussels, giving the city the unrivalled role of capital of Europe. At 10 million population, inhabited density is the second highest in Europe, after the Netherlands.

Belgium has existed in the present form only since 1830, when popular uprisings brought independence from the Netherlands. The country's name, however, dates back to a Celtic tribe, the Belgae, whom Caeser described in his commentaries as the most courageous tribe in all of Gaul.

The state recognizes and assists the Roman Catholic, Anglican and Jewish faiths. It is estimated that in the industrial and urban areas about 75 per cent of the people are Roman Catholic; in the rural areas the figure approaches 100 per cent. Although almost every individual has a strong opinion about the meaning of religion, there is not a high percentage of active members in any church. The practice of Catholicism is more strongly adhered to in Belgian Flanders, but religion remains a strong tradition for most Belgians.

Throughout its history as an independent country, a deep division has existed in Belgium between Secularists, who believe that the functions of church and state should be separated, and Roman Catholics, who advocate continuation of a stronger church role. In keeping with the progessive ideas of their time, the founders of the Belgian state stipulated in the constitution that neither the church nor state should control the other. Conflict between the two factions was particularly strong in the nineteenth century and again in the 1950s. In the political arena, the conflict has been institutionalized in the main political parties.

## ECONOMY

Economic freedom is a basic feature of the Belgian way of life. Anyone can establish a business enterprise or embark on some form of business activity. Economic life is based entirely on free enterprise and free competition. The freedom this implies is guaranteed by a number of laws and regulations governing abuses of economic power, unfair competition, exclusive sales contracts, itinerant vending, the use of brand names, the display of prices, and clearance sales.

Control over the economy is highly centralized in a small number of powerful holding companies, through direct capital participation and concentrated stockholdings. Ownership has been progressively divorced from management. The power of decision-making in the major holding companies and in large industry lies in the hands of a small group of individuals who contribute only a fraction of the capital they manage.

The public sector of the economy is relatively small. The government has a large share in banking and communications. It is principal shareholder in the Belgian airline Sabena, it plays an important role in the distribution of natural gas, and it owns the national railway system.

Belgium's economy is characterized by slow growth, high unemployment, and a high external debt. Yet the prospects for foreign goods and services remain good. Belgium is highly dependent upon foreign trade, and policies are not protectionist. Belgium's economic policy aims to improve the country's relative position – to take full advantage of the international boom cycles while sheltering the economy from downturns.

Approximately 75 per cent of Belgium's trade is with its fellow EC countries. Thus the Belgian economy is closely related to the country's economic performance. Belgium seeks to diversify and expand its trade relations with non-traditional trading partners, especially with the Middle East, Eastern Europe and China.

The Belgian government is very much aware of the need to bring about a restructuring of industry so as to make the country's exports more internationally competitive and to absorb the unemployed. Foreign, and particularly US investment, was a dynamic force in the rapid development of Belgian industry in the 1960s, and efforts have been made to continue welcoming it.

## BIBLIOGRAPHY

Deprez, Paul, 'The Low Countries', pp. 236–281 in Lee, W. R. (ed.), *European Demography and Economic Growth*. New York: St Martin's Press, 1979.

Kuraina, George Thomas, *Facts on File National Profiles. The Benelux Countries*. New York: Facts on File Publications, 1989.

Lijphart, Arend (ed.), *Conflict and Coexistence in Belgium: The Dynamics of a Culturally Divided Society* (Research Series, No. 46) Berkeley: Institute of International Studies, University of California, 1981.

Riley, R. C. and Ashworth, G. J., *Benelux An Economic Geography of Belgium, The Netherlands, and Luxembourg*. New York: Holmes and Meier Publishers, 1975.

Riley, R. C. and Ashworth, G. J., *Documents Illustrating the History of Belgium*. Brussels: Ministry of Foreign Affairs, External Trade and Cooperation in Development, 1978.

Rosselle, E. (Director General) *Annuaire Statistique de la Belgique*. Bruxelles: L'Institute Nationale de Statistique, Annual.

Rosselle, E., *OECD Economic Surveys, Belgium and Luxembourg*. Paris: Organization for Economic Cooperation and Development, 1988.

Rosselle, E., *Country Profile, Belgium and Luxembourg*. London: The Economist Intelligence Unit Limited, 1988.

# 3 Denmark

## LAND OF UNWRITTEN LAWS

Of all the European peoples, it is the Danes who are most concerned about achieving a fine balance between work and leisure, although this attention to the non-work side of life can be deceptive. Danes appear to be the most relaxed of the Scandinavians, but the Copenhagen business person is deeply serious in matters of work. The Danes enjoy the third highest standard of living in the world, and this derives from a rock-solid work ethic.

The Danish may function with great informality and friendliness, but their rules of etiquette are actually more structured than those of many other countries. An unwritten law of good manners requires the Danes to produce the easy smile, to be obliging, and never openly refuse anything. Thus, although a Dane might give an affirmative reply to a request, he might very well eventually refuse. Shakespeare made reference to the Danes: 'That one may smile and be a villain . . . it may be so in Denmark'. Villainous is certainly an overstatement today, but visitors should strive for an understanding of the nuances.

Danish families are close and stable, and they hold the belief that each individual has a right to make decisions for himself or herself. Children are brought up understanding the principles of self-reliance, and are then allowed to govern themselves. The educational system in Denmark is modern and innovative. Self-teaching, critical thinking, and teamwork are furthered at the primary level. English and German are required foreign languages, and Russian, French and Spanish are also widely studied and spoken. The literacy rate is 99 per cent.

Evangelical Lutheran is the constitutionally established church and its affairs are regulated by law. About 96 per cent of the population belongs, although attendance at services is low. The church appears to be strongest during times of crises, such as World Wars I and II.

Danish, the official language, belongs to the closely interrelated Scandinavian group of the Germanic languages. Speakers of the Danish, Norwegian and Swedish languages communicate without much difficulty.

Denmark is considered a 'low context' society. Interpersonal communications is for the most part verbal, without meaningful body language.

For example, use of the hands when communicating is virtually non-existent, in contrast to the habits of southern Europeans. Placing one's hands in the pockets during a discussion, however, may be interpreted as poor manners.

In Denmark, the handshake is the usual form of greeting – the firmer the better. As one visiting businessman puts it, 'After shaking hands with a Dane, check that all the bones in your hand are still intact'. Dealing on a first-name basis is acceptable when doing business.

Danish business people like to be complimented on Danish industry and its exports, such as Danish furniture, butter, cheese, and glassware, which are famous throughout the world. Sources of pride for the Danish business community are Burmeister & Wain, the world's biggest diesel-engine manufacturer; East Asiatic Co., a leading international trading company; A. P. Moeller, a large shipping line in Scandinavia; and Danfoss and Atlas, two of the largest exporters of refrigeration equipment.

Visiting business people should ensure that they have confirmed their appointments by mail, telex or telephone, and punctuality for business meetings is a requirement. A business card should be presented at the beginning of a meeting. A modest gift of liquor or tobacco is acceptable.

When calling on business contacts, you will find a soft-sell approach is best. Aggressive, hard-sell techniques are not tolerated.

Since Copenhagen's trading traditions go back over 1,000 years, the history and longevity of companies are well respected. If a foreign firm has a prominent background and if it has been in business for a number of decades, these facts are worth noting in conversation.

Few topics are off-limits in dealing with the Danes – food, history, and international affairs are proper areas to explore. Danes will often have a remarkable depth of knowledge of history. The topic of personal income should be avoided, as it is considered private.

It is common to be invited to dinner in a Danish home. On the first visit, it is polite to bring a gift to the woman of the house, usually a bouquet of flowers. Formal rules of etiquette are important. One should enter only when invited to do so, sit where the host suggests, and never follow the host into another room unless invited to do so. It is impolite to leave the table without asking to be excused or unless the hostess rises. Before leaving the table, a person should compliment the hostess on her meal.

The Danes have a unique way of making a toast at such occasions. When one person wants to toast another, he should raise the glass and look into the other person's eyes, pronounce the toast, drink from the glass, then look into another person's eyes, and then put the glass down.

A foreign businessman should be prepared to attend many formal black-tie events. The formal dinner starts promptly when all guests have arrived. It is not common to have cocktails before the seating. All toasts should be initiated by the host. Never begin sipping the wine until the host has tasted and approved. If platters are being passed around, it is wise to start with small portions, for one is expected to accept second and third portions. The host will only recognize that you are finished when both your fork and knife are properly placed on your plate. The dinners are often very long, and Danes will generally stay at the table long after the meal has been completed.

Decisions in business are made in much the same way as in other Western countries. In a corporation, where a decision comes from depends on the magnitude and importance of it. Major decisions are dictated by senior management, whereas middle management makes the everyday, operating decisions.

During negotiations, Danes expect the foreigner to present facts and expected outcomes. Excessive selling is not welcome, as the product or service is expected to sell itself if it is good.

When conducting business, the Danes like to be comfortable with all details of a deal. They will often insist on one more meeting just to ensure that everything is in order. Business lunches tend not to be long, and they usually wrap up everything that has already been discussed. Dinner and drinks may serve two purposes: they celebrate a finished deal or they may break the ice for a meeting the following day.

Because of the cool, rainy and windy climate, jackets are worn in daytime as well as at night. Casual clothes are acceptable for most occasions, but in semi-formal situations, dresses rather than trousers are the norm for women. It is the custom for men to wear jackets and ties to church, dinners, meetings and indoor concerts.

Do not discuss the issue of clothing nor compliment associates on his or her taste in clothes. While this may seem to be a good opener in some cultures, it is viewed as extremely odd and out of normal conversational context in Denmark.

## HISTORY AND GOVERNMENT

Denmark is a small constitutional monarchy in northwestern Europe lying between the North and Baltic seas. In history and in politics, it has been part of Scandinavia, but geographically it borders the northern part of Germany. It includes the Jutland Peninsula and about 100 inhabited islands in the Kattegat and Skagerrak Straits. The country is made up of a narrow-base peninsula and 483 islands with a total coastline of 7,000 kilometres. Most of the land is arable, and the country has no mountains or large rivers. Greenland and the Faroe Islands in the North Atlantic also are part of Denmark.

Because of its location, Denmark has been a crossroads for trade for many centuries. It was the peninsula across which the earliest human settlers moved in their journey to Sweden and Norway. In the Middle Ages, Denmark became the principal agent in the expanding trade between western and eastern Europe through the Baltic Sea; the trade increased commercial activity in Denmark itself, and this helped to make Copenhagen the major port of transit that it is today.

Denmark has served Scandinavia as a catalyst and transmitter of ideas and other cultural influences from the large European cities. From Denmark the Lutheran Protestant Reformation was introduced to Iceland and Norway. In addition, the French Enlightenment and German romanticism and nationalism reached Scandinavia through Denmark.

The government's primary role in the economy is to ensure orderly functioning of the capital markets and to provide funds for investment when the public interest is at stake and when private monies are insufficient. Although state participation in business activities has been enlarged in recent years, it is concentrated mainly in projects beyond the scope of Danish private business.

Under the Social Democrat government, the direction has been towards fewer national holdings. The government has occasionally helped failing major companies to survive to preserve jobs, but this is not its usual policy.

The government has a monopoly or a majority holding in the railways, airports and communications media. Most of the country's power stations are run and owned by the state. It also has authority over all natural resources, but the resources may be mined and developed by the private sector.

## ECONOMY

Denmark's highly developed agriculture once held an important position among the country's occupations, but by 1960 only 16 per cent of the population was employed in this type of work. However, agriculture was one of the most important factors in the historical development of Danish industry. The main areas of agriculture are grain crops, grass, root and forage crops, along with large dairy and poultry production.

Labour unions are powerful in Denmark, and the majority of them are associated with the National Trades Union Centre. Most unions are craft unions, but the largest ones are the general unions of unskilled and semi-skilled workers.

Denmark's foreign trade is mostly within Europe. European Free Trade Association (EFTA) countries make up 20 per cent of Denmark's exports and European Community (EC) countries contribute 45 per cent.

Great Britain is the largest purchaser of Danish agricultural produce, with West Germany second, these two countries buy 60 per cent of all

Denmark's agricultural products. Sweden is Denmark's biggest market for manufactured goods and its second largest market overall.

Urban centres are connected by adequate roads, and motor traffic is heavy. The number of bicycles is estimated to be over 2 million, most of them motorized. Public passenger traffic uses privately owned bus lines. The state operates most of the railway systems as well as connecting ferry services, and despite the number of automobiles, rail traffic and ferry services continue to be important modes of transportation.

Danish ships conduct almost all of the water transport between Danish ports in addition to extensive trade between foreign ports. Copenhagen is a free harbour for the shipment of cargo.

The Danish monetary unit is the krone (plural, kroner) and is denoted by the symbol D.Kr.

Two factors important to the Danish business structure are the relative small size of the country, and its lack of raw materials. Before 1958, Denmark was an agricultural society and it was not until then that industrial products for export exceeded agricultural exports.

Since 1950, agriculture's share of the work force has decreased from 21 per cent to 7 per cent, but this cutback in workers has not decreased output. However, agriculture's rising production is being offset by EEC levies, and export earnings from agriculture will grow slowly, if at all. More than half of the industrial force is employed by firms that have less than 200 employees. But Denmark is now a world leader in marine diesel and motor technology, as well as a leading supplier of cement, beer, hearing aids, thermostatic controls, merchant vessels, and industrial enzymes.

## BIBLIOGRAPHY

Denmark Statistiske Departement, *Danmarks Statistik, Statistique du Danemark*. Copenhagen: DSD, Annual.

Einhorn, Eric, *Welfare States in Hard Times: Problems, Policy and Politics in Denmark and Sweden*. Kent, Ohio: Kent Popular Press, 1982.

Melchior, Arne, *There is Something Wonderful in the State of Denmark*. Secaucus, NJ: Lyle Stuart, 1987.

Ministry of Foreign Affairs, Press and Cultural Relations Department, *Denmark: An Official Handbook*. Copenhagen: MFA, Annual.

Nordfinanz Bank, *The Scandinavian Market, A Statistical Survey of Four Scandinavian Countries*. Zurich: Nordfinanz Bank, Zurich, Annual.

Organization for Economic Cooperation and Development, *Denmark*. Paris: OECD: Annual.

Royal Danish Ministry of Foreign Affairs, *Economic Survey of Denmark*. Copenhagen: RDMFA, Annual.

## USEFUL WORDS AND PHRASES

| *English* | *Pronunciation* | *Danish* |
|---|---|---|
| Good morning | go MOHRN | God Morgen |
| Good evening | go AHF-tehn | God Aften |
| My name is . . . | mitt NOUN ehr | Mit Navn er . . . |
| Please (do something) | VAHR so ven-lee aht | Vaer so venlig at |
| Thank you | Tahk | Tak |
| Excuse me | OON-shkewl my | Undskyld mig |
| Goodbye | Far-Vill | Farvel |
| Yes | YAH | Ja |
| No | NIGH | Nej |
| I do not understand | deh FOR-STOH yaih EEK-eh | Det forstar jeg ikke |
| Today | ee DAY | I Dag |
| Tomorrow | ee MOHRN | I Morgen |
| How much does it cost? | vohr My-eht KOS-ter deh? | Hvor meget Koster det? |

# 4  Eastern Europe

## A STOREHOUSE OF PENT-UP ENERGY

An aura of nineteenth century charm survives in the manners and morals of the educated classes in East European capitals. Old-world grandeur blows through the economic ruins. Although cultures vary widely in the region, sometimes clashing violently, a common feature to them all is their passion for the past. Sooner or later, nostalgia enters any conversation with business executives, entrepreneurs, professors, artists, workers and even former Communist Party officials. Political and military upheavals throughout this century have left the East Europeans battered but not bowed.

The people tend to be openly sentimental, perhaps the more so because pent-up emotion under the sterile constraints of Communism for 45 years is now unbridled. But most of all it is the prospects for the future that keep them going. Like butterflies breaking out of their chrysallises, the people of this region are beginning to fly.

The extraordinary wave of popular revolts in the closing months of 1989 breathed new life into the area. The East Europeans are rejoining the wider community of Europe, and they desperately want to prove their worth. Still proud, they want first of all to be accepted as equals. 'Yes, we need Western help', sighed a harassed academic friend of ours in Prague who advises the new presidency on economic matters. 'But we will not accept to be treated as children. We insist on respect. We can make a good contribution to any business venture today, and a bigger one tomorrow.'

The prospects of Hungary, Poland and Czechoslovakia becoming members of the European Community are improving as democratic institutions take hold and the free market sputters into action. Given the economic hurdles ahead, however, associate EC membership in the mid-1990s is the most optimistic prognosis. Strengthening of political institutions and healthier economies would be necessary first steps.

The central preoccupation in Eastern Europe today is not political change – that has been achieved to some degree in all the countries of the region except Albania, and only requires development. At issue today is foreign investment, how to attract it and how to implement it. The entire region lags perhaps 50 years behind its Western European neighbours in living standards; upgrading the infrastructure and industrial base will require massive financial resources through to the end of this century and into the next. Morgan Stanley International has estimated the cost of reconstruction at $6–12 trillion over the next 20 years.

Degrees of backwardness range from the former German Democratic Republic (now a depressed zone of the newly unified German state) to the remote, horse-and-donkey agricultural economy of Bulgaria. Below them all is Albania, the last to come to grips with political reform and thus the laggard in launching reconstruction.

Following the political change of 1989–90, Western entrepreneurs flooded into Berlin, Warsaw, Budapest, Prague and other capitals to assess prospects. The backwardness was well known to them all, but many of the early prospectors came home stunned by the degree of neglect they observed. Conditions were worse than the East Europeans themselves had acknowledged, even in official state statistics. One German businessman told *International Management*: 'It is a long, dark tunnel, and we cannot see daylight yet'.

The mechanics of operating in Eastern Europe will evolve slowly in the coming years. Currencies must be convertible so that meaningful profit can be generated and repatriated; realists predict that cash from the West will remain a mere trickle until confidence in the area's financial and legal institutions can be established.

Opportunities for development thus remain highly problematical. The removal of Soviet hegemony in 1989 and 1990 brought many benefits to the region, but also gave rise to ancient jealousies and unresolved claims among minority peoples – perhaps the greatest threat to stability. Given the uncertainties, economic development on a large scale seems unlikely for the immediate future. In the twenty-first century, however, Eastern Europe may have a chance to converge with Western Europe in a partnership for prosperity.

## POLAND

In the depths of Stalinist rule in Eastern Europe, probably the most daring of the Soviet Union's satellite states was Poland. Strikes at the Gdansk shipyard in 1970 erupted violently, ending in the death of 300 people. The resentment smouldered for 10 years, breaking out again in 1980. This flare-up thrust Lech Walesa and his Solidarity movement into international prominence, eventually leading to democratic government and a burgeoning market economy in 1988. With the approval of Soviet President Mikhail Gorbachev the ideological ground was cleared for rapid progress. Indeed, the collapse of Communist regimes in other Eastern European countries in 1989 can be traced back to these lonely and courageous revolts by the Poles. The land of Chopin and Copernicus had regained its self-assurance.

True to form, Poland has pushed the furthest and most rapidly into market economy reforms. Prices were freed in 1990 and a privatization programme was initiated to transfer assets from the state to investors – foreign and domestic. The zloty was granted limited convertibility. The soundness of the economy was threatened by foreign debt of $40 billion, but Western investors continue to prospect the great Polish market – the largest of all the Eastern Europe countries, with a population of 37 million.

## CZECHOSLOVAKIA

The closed society of neo-Stalinism never sat easily on the Czechoslovak people. The region's rich cultural heritage, dating back to the Middle Ages, miraculously survived this century's two World Wars undamaged, preserving physical links to the great past. Some 4,000 chateaux dot the countryside, and about forty towns and cities have preserved their medieval architectural flavour. The heavy hand of central planning and the Communist Party bureaucracy clashed with the classic surroundings.

The country's more recent democratic past burned in the national memory in the 45 years since World War II. Although Czechoslovakia has existed only since 1918, national identity was quick to take form. Tomas Masaryk, the first elected President, remained a symbol of hope throughout the post-war period of Soviet domination. A brief experiment in loosening the confines of Communism in 1968 frightened the Soviet Union, however, into launching an invasion to suffocate the movement. Liberal Communist Party First Secretary Alexander Dubcek was seized by the Soviet military as a traitor, handcuffed and flown to Moscow for a personal rebuke by Soviet Party leader Leonid Brezhnev. Witnesses spoke of a tearful Brezhnev saying to Dubcek, 'Sasha, how could you?'

Czechoslovaks now recall that after 1968 they entered a long sleep, a period of 'internal exile' in which they lived a double life: superficial acceptance of their hard-line political leadership, while saving their true energy and emotion for the privacy of the home and a few trusted friends. As for their working life, they like to recall today, 'We pretended to work, and the state pretended to pay us'.

The pledge of Soviet President Mikhail Gorbachev in 1988 to allow political pluralism to flourish in Czechoslovakia gradually led the country to press for fundamental change. Emboldened by the reforms sweeping other countries of Eastern and Central Europe, a popular uprising overthrew the Communist regime of Gustav Husak in November 1989. Dissident playwright Vaclav Havel, imprisoned under Husak, became interim President, then was elected in national balloting. A year later in Moscow, a Soviet economist who advised Gorbachev on Eastern

European affairs confided to us that the Czechs had been awfully slow to make their move. 'We promised we would not react', he told us. 'They lost a year because they would not believe us.' Clearly it was the Czechs' recent history that made them hesitate.

Today the country's 16 million people are working to transform their lives and re-establish links with Western Europe. The economic priority is to restore the industrial base to Western standards through foreign investment and modern management techniques. Some exiles, including Thomas Bata, the Toronto-based manufacturer of shoes, are helping the Prague leadership finds its way back to economic health.

## HUNGARY

Scientists working on the American 'Manhattan Project', the top-secret effort that developed the first atomic bomb in World War II, were surprised and impressed by the great contribution of Hungarians on the team – Teller, Szilard, Wigner and von Neumann. In light moments, the American physicists developed the theory that Hungarians were not humans at all, they were Martians who were concealing their origins in order to avoid being hacked to death by earthlings. The proof was threefold: their language, which is unrelated to the languages of neighbouring countries; their wanderlust, which finds expression in Hungarian gypsies; and, most importantly, their unearthly intelligence, which put non-Hungarians to shame.

Hungarians, it is true, have a history of producing great achievers. In the arts, Franz Liszt and Bela Bartok left permanent traces. The Austro-Hungarian monarchy of the Habsburgs launched potent efforts to develop industry in the years immediately following creation of the joint nation in 1867. The industrial tradition survives today and is developing rapidly. Austria and Hungary were divided again after World War I, at much cost to Hungary, however. A yearning for lost territories led Hungary to align with Germany in World War II, then in 1948, under Soviet domination, Communist power was installed through the Hungarian Workers' Party.

An uprising to bring in a democratic government was crushed by the Soviets in 1956, leading to the exodus of hundreds of thousands of Hungarians, who fanned out across Western Europe and the United States. Today the Hungarian exile community numbers about 5 million. Within Hungary, the population is only about 10 million.

Experiments with increasingly bold hybrids of socialism and capitalism from the late 1950s onwards prepared Hungary best for the eventual adaptation to a free market economy. Other East Europeans looked on with envy at the 'Hungarian model', the semi-free economy also known as 'goulash Communism'. None of its neighbours could match the range of products and equipment that Hungary was marketing successfully in the West even before the true reforms were put in place: Ikarus buses, Fabulon and Helia-D cosmetics, Ganz cranes and electric meters, and Tungsram lamps for cars and trucks.

So attractive is Hungarian industry that Western investment has flowed relatively freely. After General Electric of America purchased control of Tungsram, signs of backlash against excessive foreign influence in the economy began to surface.

## ROMANIA

Romania is a great sprawling country more than twice the size of Bulgaria and Hungary combined. Rich in legend, the misty Transylvania region in the heart of the nation is the setting for the Dracula saga. The Carpathian mountain range covers about 35 per cent of the country's land mass, forming an arc around the northern and central regions. Agriculture accounts for about one-third of gross national product, giving the peasant population a strong say in the new quasi-democratic society.

But beyond these simple facts, Romania in many ways remains an enigma. Culturally, the country has great affinity with Western Europe. The language is East Europe's only Latin-based tongue, a result of its conquest at the hands of the Roman Empire in AD 106, and the intellectuals tend to speak French – indeed, they are Francophile to their fingertips. As evidence of their long struggle to avoid being swept up in the Soviet orbit, the Romanians persistently displayed the greatest resistance to Soviet domination of any of the East European group – Yugoslavia aside. For example, no Romanian troops participated in the 1968 Warsaw Pact invasion of Czechoslovakia.

With all the apparent congruence of interests with the West, it is curious that reforms have not moved in step with other East European states. The country's efforts in 1990 to join in the free-market trends in Eastern Europe have advanced only in fits and starts. After the 1989 execution of President Nicolae Ceauscescu and his wife, intellectuals took power and expected to lead the country swiftly into free elections that would repudiate all that Ceausescu stood for: megalomania, greed, and contempt for free discussion. Sporadic violence between the liberal and conservative movements has scarred the reform endeavour, resulting in a freely elected government that still practises repression by brutality. Coal miners swinging batons cleared protesters from the streets of central Bucharest in the spring of 1990, apparently in the belief they were helping prevent a coup d'état by forces more liberal than the elected government. Elected President Ion Iliescu solemnly thanked them for their bloody performance.

In these early days of political evolution, society is polarized between the liberal students and intellectuals and the law-and-order elements of the work force aided by remnants of the former *Securitate*, the former secret police. The instability has resulted in a certain reluctance among Western companies to seek opportunities there. The wavering may be attributed to three reasons: firstly, state-sponsored violence makes a poor environment for free enterprise; secondly, Romanians have been unable to project a clear consensus on the direction they wish to take or the pace of change they feel they can absorb; and, thirdly, the condition of the Romanian economy has turned out to be worse than expected.

## BULGARIA

As one of Eastern Europe's southernmost cultures, Bulgaria offers a pleasant mix of soul and warmth. Bulgarians tend to eat well, mix readily with their fellow citizens, and reflect their sunny climate in easy laughter. But history has made the country a sort of doormat. For five centuries, until 1877, the Ottoman Empire ruled the nation. In two subsequent periods, including the 45 years since the end of World War II, Russia has held sway. Mosques and Cyrillic script are everyday reminders of the country's origins.

So when democratization came to Eastern Europe in late 1989, it was as if Bulgaria had been sitting in wait, tense as a coiled spring. When the liberal trends began to spread, Bulgaria's nine million people seized the opportunity. This most loyal of Soviet client states quickly broke away from the tyranny of the Communist Party, catching even the closest Western observers unawares. One multinational country manager in Bulgaria, who had left on a year-end vacation a few days before the Party was toppled from power by public protests, had telexed his home office that he was certain of at least one thing: Bulgaria would not go down. No sooner had he landed in Britain than the Communist regime, in power since the end of World War II, fell to more liberal forces.

Emerging from domination, Bulgaria eventually promises to be an appealing place. The friendly people, the abundance of sunshine and food give it a sunbelt feeling. The process of creating a free market, however, has been impeded by the twin obstacles of market ineptitude and determination of the bureaucrats to protect their positions. Barter and countertrade deals are the main modes of exchange.

Major economic questions such as taxation, repatriation of profits and payment of personnel are still evolving and must be closely monitored while making investment decisions. The Bulgarians seem determined to move towards the free market, but will need perhaps a generation to find their way.

# YUGOSLAVIA

An assemblage of nationalists living within an uneasy alliance, Yugoslavia is a potential melting pot that won't melt. Dozens of cultures and ethnic groups are packed into the region, comprising a nation of 23 million people in search of a common identity. The ruggedly mountainous country enjoys or suffers from one of the largest number of border states in the world. The jagged 2,100-kilometre coastline on the Adriatic turns inland at Trieste as the frontier runs alongside Italy, Austria, Hungary, Romania, Bulgaria, Albania and Greece. Indeed, the artificial six-republic federation threatens periodically to break up. Yugoslavia (literally meaning Southern Slavia) is one of Eastern Europe's special cases.

The emergence of Josip Broz Tito as partisan organizer during World War II and post-war national leader was a stroke of great good fortune for the country. Tito's toughness and personal prestige held the federation together despite old disputes among the republics, and his death in 1980 left a void yet to be filled. The presidency rotates annually among nine representatives elected every four years by the National Assembly and the parliaments of the six republics. While effective in ethnic terms, it decentralizes power and slows the decision-making process.

Yugoslavia, now with a mix of 40 per cent Serbs and 22 per cent Croats, was created in the aftermath of World War I. In 1918, the kingdom that was created encompassed the Croats, Serbs and Slovenes; it adopted the name Yugoslavia in 1929. The Serbs dominated the federation until World War II. Tito established a Communist state after the war, but turned his back on Stalin in 1948.

Yugoslavia has remained non-aligned ever since, making its own rules for political and economic development, including much-publicized experiments in self-management. Stability and prosperity have been elusive, however, giving rise to violent labour strife, inflation at more than 200 per cent per year, and foreign debt of more than $20 billion. Accordingly, foreign investment has developed cautiously, as outsiders wait and see.

## BIBLIOGRAPHY

Cook, Edward and Cumming, Robert, *Eastern Europe: Agricultural Production and Trade Prospects Through 1990*. Washington, D.C.: US Government Printing Office, 1984.

Gapinski, J.H., Skegro, B. and Zuehlke, T.W., *Modeling the Economic Performance in Yugoslavia*. New York: Praeger Publishers, 1989.

International Trade Press, 1990.

Kornai, Janos, *The Road to a Free Economy: Shifting From a Socialist System: The Example of Hungary*. New York: W. W. Norton and Company, 1990.

Macesich, George (ed.), *Essays on the Yugoslav Economic Model*. New York: Praeger Publishers, 1989.

Organization for Economic Cooperation and Development, *Science, Technology and Innovation Policies, Yugoslavia*. Paris: OECD, 1988.

Storf, Otto, *Special Eastern Europe*. Frankfurt: Deutsche Bank Economics Department, 1990.

World Bank Country Study, *Poland Economic Management for a New Era*. Washington, D.C.: World Bank, 1990.

# 5 Finland

## THE PRAGMATIC NEUTRALS

The Finns have a term, untranslatable into English, that sums up their national character in a single word, *sisu*. This trait combines the odd mixture of violence and placidity inherent within the Finnish temperament, a balance of ardour, patience, industriousness, and the desire for power that has been evident throughout the country's history. So pervasive is this desire that neither history, literature nor the Finnish character can be understood without first considering *sisu* as the key ingredient.

Since the turn of the century, Finland has defied tremendous odds to retain its identity. Today it boasts the most prosperous economic conditions of all the Nordic countries. It is clear that determination, diplomacy, and *sisu* have carried this gem of the North through its perils. Finns are first of all survivors.

Finland's people have been influenced by the country's climate, geography, and economic and political conditions for centuries. Just as *sisu* has provided the nation with the impetus and courage to carry on, the inherent violence which the Finn possesses has often left him in dangerously precarious situations.

To curb this violence, Finns are notorious for turning to the State Alcohol Monopoly for a bottle of extremely rough and potent schnapps. Alcohol has traditionally relieved the internal conflict. Knowing this is important, as it is a common business ritual to enjoy libations during business negotiations. Foreign businesspersons must prepare themselves so as not to be caught off guard. Upon meeting a Finn it is not uncommon to celebrate a new friendship with party, drink and ultimately the sauna.

The Finns are a people of strong emotion and imagination. They are by nature kind-hearted, warm and welcoming to outsiders. It is easy to establish rapport with the Finns because there are no layers of formality that often accompany social interaction in other cultures. Being a 'low-context' society, Finland prides itself on the simplicity of its communicative skills. A word spoken represents a message delivered. It is not uncommon to have a Finn share with you his deepest thoughts on your first or second meeting. This warmth and open-minded trust is, however, kept in balance at all times with a protective dosage of *sisu* – kindly accepting, but always on guard.

Visitors to Finland and Sweden will note that the Finns are idealistic, often guided more by hope than by reality. The Finns and the Swedes are opposites in this respect, the Swedes being more realistic. The Swedo-Finns of Finland, distinguished today only by their language, combine the attributes of both cultures. They are less immediately warm to foreigners but in general they represent a more realistic and at times intellectually orientated group.

Culturally, Western life and thinking have infiltrated the Finnish lifestyle. Fashion, popular music and fast food from the West are trends that Finland's population have grabbed with open arms. While the traditional Finn resisted this Western pull for years – claiming that it is destructive for Finland's political position – the younger generations feel at ease with the influx of Western ideas and products.

## HISTORY AND GOVERNMENT

Finland is largely an egalitarian society, owing to an absence of the elaborate feudal system that dominated most other European countries in past centuries. Historically, the peasants were freeholders living a communal existence with each other. Living in rural villages and towns, the Finns were allotted their forest and land under a lottery-type system. It was a democratic procedure and dispersed the land-holding wealth evenly throughout the country.

Bordered by the Soviet Union, neutral Sweden and NATO member Norway, Finland has been obliged to pursue a policy of political neutrality. Perhaps as a result of the geographical squeeze, it is common to find the Finn expressing his pent-up desire for competition through athletics or local politics. The Finns pride themselves on their superior athletic abilities and have used them as a means of demonstrating their power throughout the world. Successful international athletes from Finland are revered within the country and treated as celebrities and heroes.

Politics can grow very heated with competitive debate and campaigning. Finland has striven to open as many doors with the West as possible and today uses economics and business as connecting links. The most recent trend in encouraging Western interest in Finland has been the use of the capital city of Helsinki as the gateway to the emerging Soviet Union. Since Helsinki is only 55 minutes by air from Leningrad and less than 2 hours from Moscow, Finland has chosen to promote economic and political interaction between Western nations and the Soviet Union, with Finland acting as neutral liaison between East and West.

Like all Europeans, the Finns have their own special blend of language, heritage and culture, yet the Finn fits easily and naturally into the European family. A foreigner visiting Finland might marvel at the absence of a single dominant type of person in the country.

The major subpopulations within Finland are composed of the lively and dark Karelians, who arrived in Finland from the East; the Tavasts, who originated within the central portion of Finland, and are sometimes recognized as 'typical' Finns because they are the more obviously Finnish in appearance, being short and stocky, with pale round faces, light hair, and pale blue eyes; and from the west, the taller, slenderer, more Nordic types, the Swedo-Finns, many of whom have continued to speak Swedish. Finland prides itself on its cultural diversity and considers itself a bit of a Northern European melting pot.

For years the issue of an 'official' language within Finland has been controversial. For centuries the Swedish-speaking Finns represented the educated elite. While they did interact (often reluctantly) with the pure Finn, this division in social class eventually led to resentment between the Swedo-Finn and the pure Finn. All that remains of the issue today, for the most part, is the language issue. Since the difference between Finnish and Swedish is greater than the difference between German and French, it is clear why this difference in languages has taken its toll on the people. Today 94 per cent of the population speak Finnish, leaving the minority Swedo-Finns, representing approximately 350,000 people, speaking Swedish.

## ECONOMY

Finland is wealthy in land, labour, and natural resources, and blessed with a strong work ethic. The country's economic future will depend upon the management and development of creative initiative and entrepreneurial spirit.

Companies in both the agricultural and industrial sectors have claimed their fortunes through successful export departments and good production quality and efficiency. Today the dynamics of international trade and a closely intertwined global economy have heightened competition. Some large companies are laying off employees in order to cope with the growing pressures.

The hope for the future lies perhaps with the smaller companies and a renewed entrepreneurial spirit. The important aspect of economic survival, critical to the Finns, lies in the support and promotion of local and regional economies within the country. Development of these economies will provide jobs and promote the growth of the domestic economy for the Finns.

## BIBLIOGRAPHY

Finnish Foreign Trade Association, *Finland: Towards the 1990s.* Helsinki: Finnish Foreign Trade Association, 1986.

MacDonald, Greg, *The Nordic Countries and Multinational Enterprises: Employment Effects and Foreign Direct Investment.* Geneva: International Labour Office, 1989.

Price Waterhouse, *Information Guide: Finland.* New York: Price Waterhouse, 1980.

Turner, Barry, *The Other European Community: Integration and Cooperation in Nordic Europe.* New York: St. Martin's Press, 1982.

Turner, Barry, 'Finland: Its Economy and Environment', *OECD Observer,* June–July 1988, p.34(4).

Woker, Daniel, *Die Skandinavischen Neutralen: Prinzip und Praxis der Schwedischen und der Finnischen Neutralitat.* Berne: P. Haupt, 1978.

# 6 France

## THE COMBATIVE LIBERTARIANS

The French are a proud, patriotic, sardonic people driven by a clear sense of their own greatness. A grand history of conquest and achievement has left its traces in the national character. With giants such as Voltaire, Montaigne, Diderot and Pasteur in their past, the French display intellectual vigour and a taste for argument as perhaps their most striking traits. Indeed, a Frenchman is more likely to be interested in a person who disagrees with him than one of like-minded views.

Yet more than most peoples of Europe, the French abound in contradictions. They profess lofty ideals of fraternity and equality, but at times give in to the most extreme selfish materialism. High priorities among the professional classes in France today are such things as owning a car and a country house, and preparing to cash in on a generous retirement scheme. At the same time, they appreciate industriousness and devotion to work, yet they are seldom willing to sacrifice the enjoyment of life out of excessive dedication to work. *Qualité de la vie* is what matters.

Above all else, the French value personal honour and integrity. One's word, when extended, may count more than any written contract.

In the background of French life at all levels looms the stubborn issue of immobility. Social standing remains important (although decreasingly so among the new breed of young managers), despite the talk of equality. French people automatically categorize themselves along the lines of their professional activities (teachers, doctors, lawyers, craftsmen, foremen, farmers), as well as their political opinions (conservative, centrist, leftist). Social interactions are thus profoundly affected by these social stereotypes.

Worse yet, status depends to a great degree on family origins. Outward signs of social status are the individual's level of education, a tasteful house or flat, and knowledge of literature and fine arts. But the all-important structure within which the system operates depends on each individual's family origins.

The structure of business in France is remarkable for the extent of family firms. A large proportion of all business is family owned, run, or dominated through major shareholdings. Unless extraordinarily gifted with some unique talent, an individual's business career depends to a great degree on family connections. In the past several years, however, there has been a tendency to hire and promote managers who are graduates of business schools.

Top executives are strongly autocratic in their style of management, and are likely to consolidate their power through picking close associates as their subordinates. These executives practise strict 'top-down' management, voicing their wishes to subordinates who then further transmit them down the line.

Procedures for conducting business in France parallel those in Western Europe and other parts of the developed world. The first business meeting or initial contact takes place with the appropriate opposite business level party, and an attempt is made to establish rapport. The business being proposed is discussed after a time, but only in an introductory fashion. No attempt should be made to reach conclusions before trust has been established.

Careful attention and interpretation should be made to all verbal responses, for French executives like to avoid written guarantees and promises in preference to verbal ones. Subsequent meetings may go directly to the matter at hand, but it is wise at the outset to understand that a business transaction in France is going to take a great deal of time, as the French are generally more systematic and deliberate than their foreign counterparts.

French cuisine is the world standard, and French managers enjoy a business lunch or dinner. Meals may consist of six or more courses, commonly lasting two or three hours. An appreciation of food and wine always enters into dinner conversation at some point. Ignorance of the subject will leave the visitor isolated.

Actual eating is performed in the Continental manner, with the left hand continuously holding the fork, while the right holds the knife. Fruits are peeled with a knife, and the delicious baguette bread is broken with the fingers (not cut with a knife), and is often used to wipe a plate.

The French language is considered a treasure and a source of pride and pleasure. Foreigners who can speak even halting French are much appreciated, but only a firm grasp of the language will make the visitor entirely welcome. Many French business people speak German and Italian, as well as English and other languages, but they much prefer to speak French at home.

Personal behaviour is a combination of direct communication and physical restraint. Eye contact, for example, indicates a sense of trust in the individual. But when addressing a superior, restraint is in order: it is wise not to add distracting body mannerisms, instead concentrating on the verbal message being delivered. Slapping of the back, or any other part of the anatomy, is strictly taboo. Handshakes are frequent. One should never address another person with hands in the pockets.

This shortlist of do's and don't's may help facilitate relationships:

- Avoid red roses and chrysanthemums when sending flowers.
- Don't put elbows on the table.
- Be prompt.
- Don't use toothpicks, combs, or nail clippers in public.
- Shake hands with a single quick shake.
- When ending a visit, wait for a polite silence before rising.
- Wait for an answer when you knock, before entering a room or office.
- 'Dropping in' is not appropriate; wait to be invited or telephone ahead to apprise people of your plans.
- Respect the French notion of business secrecy.
- In general, be conservative.

In general, a polite and respectful attitude towards business counterparts is appreciated above all else. Depending upon the business rank, one either takes the initiative in the business discussion or follows the superior's lead. All discussions are conducted in an orderly fashion. Overtly aggressive business attitudes are neither prized nor conducive to business harmony. Knowledge of whom to contact, and when to make the approach, are valued qualities.

Arguments should be avoided whenever possible in favour of compromise; but a strong argument, if respectfully submitted, will reach the right ear. An individual's sense of self-respect is most important, and one should not seek to denigrate another's standing in the business community.

In French companies, the reduced emphasis on delegation of responsibility usually means there will be less personal accountability and therefore a more rigid organizational structure. As a consequence, decision-making is often centralized, sometimes slowing the process. This may be a source of frustration for those unaccustomed to working with French firms.

Depending upon the area of business, there is apt to be some government participation in any business negotiations.

The French are exceedingly formal, using titles instead of names, especially in upward communication. Last-name usage continues in the absence of titles to a large extent, with first names usually reserved for close friends. This formality adds a degree of stability to the social encounter, as it provides the necessary information for all parties to know where the other stands in the social/work hierarchy. Politeness matters a great deal.

Introductions between two unrelated parties will be greatly aided if specific reference can be made to a third party known and trusted by the individuals.

In general, some degree of small talk should precede any business, even if it should consist only of talk of sports, travel, or the inevitable weather. When addressing superiors, keep a polite and respectful social distance at all times to avoid seeming overly familiar.

Formality applies to dress and personal appearance as well. Business and casual clothing in France are of a more form-fitting style and cut with much attention paid to choice of tasteful ties and accessories.

Ordinarily a business engagement would not include entertainment by the French at home, this being regarded as an intrusion of business into what they consider as their private family life. But if invited to dine at a French home, arrive promptly. Send flowers ahead or bring them with you – but not roses or chrysanthemums. All foods served should be sampled and consumed, with compliments perhaps being delivered on the preparation. Thank-you notes should follow a dinner or any social event, preferably the next day.

While dining, the French appreciate animated, even combative, conversation almost as much as the food itself. Topics suitable for the social setting are the arts, literature, history, and especially the cinema. Avoid competing for conversational repartee in simple matters, for the French are proven masters of the art.

Business discussions over dinner may include government or politics. Topics to avoid include family members and matters, personal income, private investments or personal political opinion. Toasts may be exchanged at any part of the meal, and are generally made in favour of one's success, health, or good fortune. Good table manners should prevail at all times, such as rising upon the entrance and exit of a female or senior male.

The attitudes of the French towards work depend on whether they are employed in the public sector or in the private sector. In the French bureaucracy and in state companies, there is often little incentive to be productive. Quotas are rarely assigned, and it is rare to lay off or dismiss employees on the basis of job performance. In the private sector, the situation is different. French managers and other employees usually work hard during their allotted working time and they have the reputation of being productive.

## HISTORY AND GOVERNMENT

France is the largest country in Western Europe, sharing boundaries with Belgium, Luxembourg, Germany, Switzerland, Italy, Monaco and Spain.

The government is dominated by a strong presidency, under which a prime minister and bicameral parliament administer affairs of government. The presidency is a seven-year term, Europe's longest. The French government is one of the leading backers of the plans to integrate the economies of the twelve nations of the European Community (EC). French statesmen, aware of their ancestors' ambitions, intend to shape and lead the process. A history of military and political adventure in the eighteenth and nineteenth centuries lives on in French character today. The ideals of the French Revolution were revived in the 1989 bicentenary celebrations, further focusing attention on the country's dramatic past.

Since the end of World War II and the end of the colonial era, France has taken in great numbers of immigrants, chiefly from North Africa (Algeria). Foreigners, who make up about 7 per cent of the population, tend to cluster in the high-employment areas such as Paris, whose foreign population has now reached 19 per cent.

## ECONOMY

A wave of denationalization has reduced the government's role in the marketplace, but France remains top-heavy with state banks and industrial enterprises. The government is the largest employer, with a budget which represents more than 20 per cent of the gross national product. France is Europe's largest food producer, and is a leading developer of technology. Services account for some 60 per cent of gross domestic product.

Provided that foreign investment in France is properly made and registered pursuant to regulations, there is no restriction on the repatriation of capital, or on the payments of dividends, royalties, loan interest, service fees, to others as long as the transactions are openly conducted. Regional and local controls exist for direct investment in particular areas of the country. The franc's exchange rate is allowed to fluctuate by up to 2.25 per cent within the European Monetary System (EMS).

Some 90 per cent of the population is Roman Catholic, slightly over 2 per cent are Protestant, 3 per cent are Moslem and 1 per cent is Jewish.

Air, railway, and highway systems are highly developed in France. Buses and taxis are relatively plentiful, with rental cars and private plane service easily obtainable. In Paris, the metro or subway is the most advanced and cleanest in the world.

The month of August is to be avoided if possible for any business travel plans without benefit of reservations, as this is the usual time for holidays. The French take 80 per cent of their vacation between 14 July and 31 August.

## BIBLIOGRAPHY

Amadon, Jean, *Les Yeux au Fond de la France*. Paris: Editions J'ai Lu, 1984.

Bremond, J., *L'Economie Française: Face aux Défis Mondiaux: Faits, Chiffres, Analyses*. Paris: Hatier, 1985.

Christian, Pierre, and Lefebvre, Philippe. *Comprendre la France*, New York: Charles Scribner and Sons, 1970.

Dandelot, Marc and Froment-Meurice, Francois, *France*. Paris: La Documentation Française, 1975.

Devaud, Marcelle and Levy, Martine, 'Women's Employment in France: Protection or Equality?', *International Labour Review*, November–December 1980, pp. 739–53.

Godt, Paul, *Policymaking in France: From de Gaulle to Mitterand*. New York: Pinter Publishers, 1989.

Harris, P. and Moran, R., *Managing Cultural Differences*. Houston, Texas: Gulf Publishing Company, 1981.

Herzog, Philippe, *Europe 1991: Construier Autrement et Aute Chose: Face a un Marche de Dupes*. Paris: Messidor/Ed. Sociales, 1989.

Hough, J. R., *The French Economy*. New York: Holmes and Meier, 1982.

House, John William, *France: An Applied Geography*. London: Methuen, 1978.

Knox, Edward, *Plus ca Change: La France Enter Heir et Demain*. Washington, DC: Hatier-Didier, 1987.

Michaud, Guy, *Le Nouveau Guide France: Manuel de Civilization Française*. Paris: Hachette, 1982.

Michaud, Guy, *Francexport*. Paris: Centre Française du Commerce Extérieur, Annual.

Naudin, Odile, *Loubards sans Fards*. Paris: Casterman, 1982.

Ross, George, *et al. (eds)*, *The Mitterrand Experiment: Continuity and Change in Modern France*. New York: Oxford University Press, 1987.

Santoni, Georges (ed.), *Société et Culture de la France Contemporaine (Contemporary French Culture and Society)*. Albany: State University of New York Press, 1981.

Wright, Gordon, *France in Modern Times: From the Enlightenment to the Present* (4th ed.). New York: Norton, 1987.

# 7  Germany

## A UNITED GERMANY AND AN INDUSTRIAL POWERHOUSE

On 3 October 1990 the black, red and gold flag of a united Germany was hoisted, ending 41 years of national division. Many German people are saying *'wir sind ein volk'* (We are one people) and the unification in name, as well as in monetary, economic and social terms, has taken place. However, the peoples of what were once East and West Germany have in many ways grown apart. One nation composed of two peoples is working towards integration.

The two Germanies evolved into two very different entities. The Federal Republic of Germany in the West was prosperous and democratic. The German Democratic Republic in the East was impoverished and undemocratic. The political, social and economic gulfs that have formed in the past four decades must be skilfully bridged to enable all to work towards the future of Germany as one united nation.

Although the Germanies are now 'socially one', many rifts can be seen. In many cases the East Germans are viewed as foreigners by their Western counterparts. The historical and linguistic ties remain, but the long separation unavoidably resulted in two very different peoples, values and beliefs. The East was smothered under Soviet hegemony, while the people in the West have benefited from the social and economic miracles of the past 40 years. The industry in the East is in ruins and pollution runs rampant, while the local administration has been generally chaotic. A worker in the East produces only 40 per cent of the output of a Western worker. Within the next few years, one-third of all East German companies are expected to close and others will require government assistance to stay open. In addition, rising unemployment will plague the East, along with rising prices and rents. The united Germany will no doubt feel the pressures and strains of the 'baggage' of its Eastern partners. However the correct plans and strategies, and the effort of all Germans, can result in time in a very prosperous and powerful nation.

The modern West German citizen is a firm believer in *Feierabend*, the doctrine of hard work during normal business hours, but an elaborate non-business life in the evenings. A high standard of living in the past two decades has allowed most West Germans to develop extensive interests beyond their professional lives. The average German is very protective of his private life and hence his leisure time.

A passion for organization prevents the typical German from being spontaneous. The tendency is to organize the time allotted for an activity – work or relaxation – to optimum efficiency, then keep as closely as possible to the fixed schedule. The manager's day tends to be well planned.

As a general rule, the Germans do not like to talk about work outside the office. But if an evening dinner appointment is business-related, discussion of work is appropriate.

Germans are free-thinking and wide-ranging in their interests. Little is excluded from an evening's discourse – religion, politics, sexual trends, and nuclear power are all fair game. The more substance and controversy, the better. Only topics relating to one's private life should be avoided. Good judgement in weighing the situation must be applied, but generally Germans enjoy a lively, informal conversation on any of the important topics of the day.

Yet in many respects they are not an outgoing people. They are close to only a few friends and relatives. The German language reflects this trait in its differentiation between acquaintance (*Bekannter*) and friend (*Freund*). The German will only use *Freund* when he really means it, otherwise it is a *Bekannter*. Close family ties are also cherished.

In business, Germans have a well-earned reputation for efficiency. They pride themselves on having top-quality products to offer on the world markets.

However, the products of Eastern Germany do not have the same reputation. In general, they are of poor quality, and this will remain a serious problem for some time. But there is an excellent education system which will give Germany in the East the confidence it needs to change rapidly, and to work effectively with foreign customers or partners.

They are formal in their business dealings, not only with foreigners but among themselves. For the visitor, it is best to be conservative and subdued, unless given the indication to be more informal. The Germans have no respect for the pushy, brassy, loud and slick salesman. Such styles indicate a weakness in the company, person, or product.

To the Germans, it is a sign of bad business or bad preparation when discussion over price leads the seller to drop the price several times in an attempt to gain the sale at any cost. Generally the Germans are more structural and rigid in their dealings. They feel they have developed a quality product and have set a fair price for it.

Maximizing profitability is not always the German's first priority. As in the case of many other Europeans, Germans often feel that the firm has a responsibility to society and the environment.

A key element in the decision-making process in Germany is the participation of the workers' council. This body represents the workers in their dealings with management, and has the power to accept or reject important strategic or investment proposals.

The workers elect representatives to the supervisory board of the firm and the board members elect the members of the executive board, which is the highest authority in the firm. Labour then has direct input into the decision-making process at all levels.

Personal relations in Germany are tradition-bound and more formal than in many other European cultures. A firm handshake is an important part of the initial greeting. Germans shake hands often, at the first greeting of the day, and also at the conclusion of a conversation. Generally the older person, or the person of higher authority, will extend the hand first. The woman extends her hand first, unless the man holds a higher position. A verbal response also accompanies the handshake.

Men should bow slightly from the shoulders and neck while greeting another person. If one is a guest entering a room filled with many people, one should proceed around the room shaking each person's hand. A friendly 'Good morning' or 'Good day' is appropriate.

Refrain from using first names. *Herr, Frau,* or, where appropriate, a professional title is fitting. Women in business should always be called *Frau,* regardless of marital status. In title-conscious Germany, proper etiquette often requires addressing individuals by their titles. Those who have attained their academic doctorate are addressed as 'Herr Doktor Schmidt', for example, or 'Frau Doktor Braun'. A friend or associate should introduce a newcomer to a group, as the Germans prefer third-party introductions.

In many countries of Europe it is common to entertain clients or future partners in the evening, perhaps at a fashionable restaurant, while business negotiations are under way. But in Germany, particularly in corporations that deal in large contracts, the general practice is to avoid any such invitations. The rule is intended to protect one against conflict of interest or a loss of *unabhangigkeit,* objectivity. Once the contract has been signed, it is an excellent idea to invite your partner or client out to dinner. At this point, the gesture will be appreciated as a reinforcement of the relationship and an implicit pledge to remain in close contact.

Germans like to think in terms of the next contract even while negotiating the current one. Long-range plans and goals are always in their minds. Many German firms that deal with foreigners complain that once a deal has been completed, the foreign partner is never heard from again. Follow-up contacts can be worth the trouble: they offer an opportunity for quality control and they keep the door open for future business.

If you receive an invitation to a German home, remember that it is an unusual honour. Be punctual. Cocktail time is usually just long enough for a quick drink. It is customary to bring a small gift of flowers to show appreciation. Avoid red roses in Germany, as in most other European countries, as they indicate romantic love. Flowers should be presented in odd numbers – five, seven or nine – to allow a symmetrical arrangement. It is proper to remove wrappings from the flowers before presenting them to the hostess.

Smoking is permissible before dining but is frowned upon during the meal. It is best not to initiate smoking, but to wait for your host to offer you a cigarette or cigar. Conversation is sometimes more formal during the meal, but is more lively and spontaneous afterwards.

Germans tend to be restrained in their body movements when talking. They do not wave their arms about in the manner of southern Europeans. It is considered rude to sit with the soles of one's shoes visible to another person, so that German men will often cross their legs at the knees rather than resting an ankle on the other knee. Erect, posture is important to a German, both while standing and sitting.

Germans like to dress well. Business attire is a conservative suit with well polished shoes. The Germans take pride in their appearance, and do not hesitate to spend time and money looking their best. Women should use cosmetics and jewelery sparingly.

## HISTORY AND GOVERNMENT

After World War II, the Allied forces divided Germany into two countries. West Germany existed in that state from 1945 until 3 October 1990. The Federal Republic of Germany is now composed of ten states, and, since the reunification on 3 October, five new states have been added, including Berlin. The five new states are called FNL (*Fuenf Neue Laender*).

The population of Germany is nearly 80 million. The terrain is relatively flat in the north, rising gradually in the south. The climate is temperate.

There are two main governing bodies in Germany, the Bundestag (Parliament) and the Bundesrat (Federal Council). The Bundestag, the larger of the two, is composed of elected representatives from the states, including Berlin, and holds the legislative power. The Bundesrat has non-voting status, although it can exercise a veto in matters concerning *Laender* (the states') interests. Germany has a president, but the position is one of honour and formality, not power. The real power lies in the office of Chancellor (*Bundeskanzler*). The Chancellor is either the leading representative of the party with a majority of seats in the Bundestag, or the leader of the largest party in a coalition government.

Although some of Germany's past can be seen in the old cities and buildings, much of the country is very modern. Germany has risen from the rubble of post-war years to become the third largest industrial power in the Western world, after the United States and Japan. Germany is the largest exporter in the world.

The Roman Catholic Church (45 per cent) and the German Protestant Church (45 per cent) account for the bulk of religious affiliations. Other denominations are grouped together in what the Germans call *Sekte* (sects). Church activity in general has dropped over the years, although both churches remain powerful and influential. There is no clear separation of church and state as in most other European countries.

Hundreds of dialects and local variations of the German language are spoken throughout the countryside, although generally in less formal situations with friends. *Hochdeutsch*, or High German, is found in all mass media. In a business context, your counterpart will avoid dialects. English is the major foreign language taught in Germany. Most internationally oriented business people can converse in English.

## ECONOMY

Three forces heavily influencing the structure of business in Germany today are the European Community (EC), co-determination, and government involvement. Germany is one of the original members of the EC. Much of German business practice is directly tied to the regulations and directives from Brussels.

The principle of collective good is important in the idea of co-determination (*Mitbestimmung*), which allows for worker participation in the management of the firm. Any firm of over five employees should have a workers' council (*Betriebsrat*) representing employees and helping them solve various grievances with management. Any coal or steel firm with more than 2,000 workers is required to have 50 per cent of the company's supervisory board composed of workers.

Germany is committed to a free enterprise economy, but government and business work closely together. The government and the major banks also hold equity participation in many firms. In public services, the railways and the post and telecommunications systems are state controlled. The state also owns a trade monopoly in alcohol.

The Germans are among the highest paid workers in the world and enjoy a comfortable standard of living. They can afford the luxuries and extras of life. An important part of this concept is the vast welfare state which supports the German worker. This includes liberal pensions, bonuses, medical and dental care, and five to six weeks of paid vacation, (two and one half days per month is required by law).

Though taxes are heavy, this system has relieved the typical German from many financial worries. The integration resulting from a united Germany is expected to ease tensions on the economy for the next few years.

## BIBLIOGRAPHY

Ardagh, John, *Germany and the Germans: An Anatomy of Society Today*. New York: Harper and Row, 1987.

Berghahn, Volker Rolf, *Modern Germany: Society, Economy, and Politics in the Twentieth Century* (2nd ed.). New York: Cambridge University Press, 1987.

Gerschenkron, Alexander, *Bread and Democracy in Germany*. Ithaca, New York: Cornell University Press, 1989.

Hartrich, Edwin, *The Fourth and Richest Reich*. New York: Macmillan, 1980.

Kahler, Erich (Robert and Rita Kimber, (eds), *The Germans*. Boulder, Colorado: Westview Press, 1985.

Katzenstein, Peter J. (ed.), *Industry and Politics in West Germany: Toward the Third Republic*. Ithaca, NY, Cornell University Press, 1989.

Lipschitz, Leslie, and Kremers Jeroen and McDonald, Donogh, *The Federal Republic of Germany, Adjustment in a Surplus Country*. Washington, DC: IMF, 1990.

Marsh, David, *The Germans: A People at the Crossroads*. New York: St Martin's Press, 1990.

Mattox, Gale and Vaughan John (eds.), *Germany Through American Eyes: Domestic and Foreign Policy Issues*. Boulder: Westview Press, 1988.

Organization for Economic Cooperation and Developement, *Regional Policies in Germany*. Paris: OECD, 1989.

Owen, Smith E., *The West German Economy*. New York: St Martin's Press, 1983.

Phillips, John, *Coping with Germany*. New York: B. Blackwell, 1989.

Romer, Karl (ed.), *Facts About Germany*. Gutersloh: Lexikothek, 1980.

Tietmeyer, Hans and Guth, Wilfried. *Two Views of German Reunification*. Washington, DC: Group of Thirty, 1990.

Turner, Henry Ashby, *The Two Germanys since 1945*. New Haven: Yale University Press, 1987.

# 8    Great Britain

## EUROPE'S ECCENTRICS

Britain's love of eccentricity is usually explained by the long-term effects of island fever – the physical separation of British culture from the influence of its European neighbours. Britain's motorists are the last in Europe to drive on the left and such pleasures as fine cuisine are viewed as French affectations. In casual speech, Britain is rarely referred to as part of Europe, rather as an entity unto itself. 'I'm off to Europe today', a British businessperson will say while boarding a British Airways flight to Paris.

Indeed, in some extreme cases the Continentals are thought to be an irrelevant subspecies morally inferior and incapable of speaking proper English. To drive this point home, the British stubbornly mispronounce French place names, as if to show the French the error of their ways. Beauchamps becomes 'Beechams', Beaulieu becomes 'Bewley', and Boulogne becomes 'Boo-loyne'.

Some of the peculiar charm of isolation is beginning to wane, however, as Britain enters a period of adaptation to the rigours of the world economy. The world's thirty-seventh largest country will not be competitive on its own. The class system is giving way to a meritocracy, and younger British achievers are breaking free of tradition. By the mid-1990s, the Eurotunnel will finally link Britain to the Continent.

Business achievement today is regarded as a goal worth pursuing. For the first time, business leaders rival the aristocracy in prestige.

Doing business in Britain requires sensitivity to the country's grand past and more recent decline. Above all, the British value their privacy and may resent inquiries regarding their families or work situations. Safe topics include the weather, sports, music or other subjects pertaining to local cultural life. The British are great lovers of their country, although they do not openly admit it. The monarchy remains widely regarded as a permanent, positive feature of the establishment, and as such is not a suitable subject for jest by foreigners.

While in a business environment, visitors should not be too casual or relaxed. Feet should always be kept off the furniture, and legs should not be conspicuously crossed. Men should keep their jackets closed, and exposing too much shirt is considered uncouth. Loud voices are rude, and shouting across open spaces is improper. Be careful not to interrupt another person's conversation.

In any public speech, as in private, the visitor can establish rapport with the audience by emphasizing the positive aspects of Britain's influence in world affairs. Humour is welcome, but only if it is natural. Never recite jokes out of a joke book.

The British executive does not get under way early in the morning. The working breakfast is gaining acceptance and should be suggested only tentatively. Nor should the visitor assume that the British business person would want to participate in a long lunch. In London clubs, business discussions are often taboo, and business papers are expressly forbidden. Waiters will not hesitate to reprimand offenders. Food quality in most clubs is considered of little importance. Indeed, a reverse snobbery sometimes takes over – the simplicity and blandness become the butt of good-humoured banter. At the root of this curious practice is often a nostalgia for the institutional food of the British boarding school. French visitors in particular have problems appreciating the low priority of careful food preparation.

Business dinners can be useful for public relations purposes but not for actual business negotiations. Invite wives along only if a friendship is blooming.

The British tend to be insular and haughty. Keeping in mind the aversion to expressing strong feelings, your initial greeting should be restrained. A handshake is the customary form of introduction but it should not be overly aggressive. Backslapping or any other form of physical display is considered improper.

While young people or friends often address each other by first names, it is best to use titles and family names in order to show respect. The exception is the use of 'Sir', which is employed with the first name, as in 'Sir James', not 'Sir Goldsmith'.

The British tend to be deferential towards superiors, and this often requires keeping one's appropriate distance, both literally and figuratively. In conversation, British gestures are restrained and do not exhibit excessive feeling or emotion, so that a conservative manner will win a measure of respect. A visiting business person should not show ostentatious friendliness. Demonstrative hand gestures or excessive physical contact should be avoided.

The British tend to be tolerant of other people's points of view and therefore compromise is a very important tool in negotiations. Generally, if there is a problem the British response is to form a committee to jointly solve it. Decisions are often postponed, but when they are finally made, they are in most cases based on an easy compromise. Directly related to this tolerance is the British notion of fair play.

It is considered distasteful to haggle over a fee or any matter concerning money. Finances are not a favourite topic of conversation and will sometimes half-jokingly be dismissed as the 'sordid subject of coin'. The typical business person does not perceive work as the ladder to success, yet hard work and honesty are key elements of the culture. The key in Britain is not to be seen to be striving too hard (although discreet striving is quite acceptable).

The British do not equate time with money, but they do expect visitors to be punctual and obey the rules regarding proper times for activities (e.g. tea/coffee time). The pace of life is controlled. One should not attempt to rush negotiations or business meetings.

As in most other respects, the British style of dress is more conservative than in many areas of the world. A dark suit should be worn for all business and social engagements. Extremely informal clothing is not considered appropriate even during leisure activities.

No doubt because of the country's former social structure, the British still maintain subtle differences in dress, especially for social events. For the male traveller who may find himself improperly equipped for weekend invitations to the country, advice on proper attire is worth seeking. To a foreigner, a hacking jacket looks much like a sports coat, but to a gentleman, there is a world of difference.

Some helpful tips on etiquette:

- A striped tie should not be worn, as it may be similar to a British regimental tie.
- The term 'British' is usually preferable to 'English' (don't forget about Scotland and Wales – not to mention Northern Ireland).
- The best personal approach is formal and low-key.
- Observe two breaks during the course of the day: a morning coffee break and an afternoon tea break.
- British business person often limit entertaining to a club or restaurant. Do not be offended if you are not invited home.
- At lunch or dinner, gin and tonic or sherry are served before meals, while wine accompanies meals. Coffee is served after meals.
- It is inappropriate to be disrespectful of the Crown.

As with business appointments anywhere in Europe, one should also be punctual. The same applies for special engagements. If visiting a family, be prepared for a handshake at the door. When invited for dinner, flowers or chocolates should be presented openly to the lady of the house upon arrival. Compliments regarding the decor are in order. Guests should always thank the host for his hospitality and thank the lady of the house for the meal upon departure. In addition, it is important to write a thank-you note following any social function.

At formal engagements, the Queen is often toasted and smoking is banned before the toast.

The utmost in fine manners must be displayed at all times. Men should always hold doors open for women and stand when women enter the room; on a bus that is full, a gentleman should offer his seat to a woman, to an invalid, or to an older person.

## HISTORY AND GOVERNMENT

Great Britain (originally named so as to distinguish it from Brittany, across the channel in France) measures only 480 kilometres across and just under 960 kilometres between the north and the south coasts. No point on the island is more than 120 kilometres from the sea.

The country has relatively few natural resources, with the exception of coal reserves and North Sea oil and gas. Although 80 per cent of the country is arable land, Britain is only able to produce just over one half of the nation's food requirements.

A long tradition of foreign conquest and domination of the seas is therefore justified by the British as a pragmatic necessity. Although the empire has crumbled rapidly in this century, memories of grandeur, much as in France, linger in the national character.

An unhealthy rivalry still disturbs Britain's ties with France. Former Prime Minister Thatcher dismissed the importance of the freedoms gained in the French Revolution, for example, claiming that Britain created the concept of equality with the signing of the Magna Carta at Runnymede in 1215.

Despite the fact that the country is as far north as Newfoundland, the climate is mild and temperate due to the tropical Gulf Stream which sweeps over Britain from the Caribbean. This warm-weather current provides Britain with a relatively moist climate, but, contrary to popular opinion, it is not an excessively rainy one.

The population of the United Kingdom is approximately 56 million and has shown very little growth since 1974. Britain has one of the highest population densities in the world – 500 persons per square mile. Although only 8 per cent of the nation's area can be termed urban, approximately 91 per cent of the population resides in the city and suburban regions. One third of the population lives in the seven major areas of London, Birmingham, Glasgow, Leeds, Liverpool, Sheffield, and Manchester. Of the total population, 83 per cent are English, 9 per cent are Scottish, and 5 per cent are Welsh. The Irish comprise only 3 per cent.

The primary religion in the United Kingdom is Protestant with approximately 27 million people belonging to the Church of England, known colloquially as the C of E. About 9 per cent of the population is Roman Catholic, and there are substantial Islamic communities made up of unassimilated immigrants from India, Pakistan and other former colonies.

The literacy rate is 99 per cent and local education authorities provide public schooling from primary to university level. Full-time education is compulsory to the age of 16, but only about 6 per cent go on to university.

The government, a constitutional monarchy, is composed of a body of ministers who are the leading members of the political party in power and are responsible to parliament. They act in the name of the sovereign. Elections are held at the discretion of the prime minister but must be called before the expiration of a five-year electoral mandate. The prime minister may ask the monarch to call a general election any time.

## ECONOMY

The British government continues to provide an open-door policy towards foreign investment and offers selective incentives for companies wanting to establish or expand manufacturing operations. Japanese manufacturers have been especially clever in taking advantage of tax and training incentives. Any foreign capital investment which creates employment and imports technological and managerial skills is welcomed, but when the investment is perceived as being the cause of increased unemployment or when decisions are made overseas without sufficient regard for the interests of the resident workers, conflict can result. The wave of Japanese investment in the late 1980s has been criticized on these grounds.

The government is giving priority to industrial development in order to reverse the relative decline in the industrial sector.

The Department of Industry is responsible for industrial policy as a whole on both the national and the regional level. Furthermore, there is a close association between commerce and the government through such channels as the National Economic Development Council and the Economic Development Committees.

The central body representing British business and industry is the Confederation of British Industry (CBI), which is recognized by the government as a channel for consultation between the public and the private sector.

## BIBLIOGRAPHY

Bogdanor, Vernon, *The People and the Party System: The Referendum and Electoral Reform in British Politics*. New York: Cambridge University Press, 1981.

Briggs, Asa, *A Social History of England*. New York: Viking Press, 1984.

Bulmer-Thomas, Victor (ed), *Britain and Latin America: A Changing Relationship*. New York: Cambridge University Press, 1989.

Capie, Forrest, *Depression and Protectionism: Britain between the Wars*. London and Boston: G. Allen and Unwin, 1983.

Central Office of Information, *Britain, An Official Handbook*. London: HMSO, Annual.

Hill, Malcolm R., *EastWest Trade, Industrial Cooperation, and Technology Transfer: The British Experience*. Aldershot, Hants: Gower, 1983.

Kurian, George Thomas, *Facts on File National Profiles: The British Isles*. New York: Facts on File, 1990.

Laslett, Peter, *The World We Have Lost: Further Explored*. New York: Scribner, 1984.

Owen, Richard, *The Times Guide to 1991: Britain in a Europe Without Frontiers: Comprehensive Handbook*. London: Times Books, 1990.

Rowthorn, Bob, *De-industrialization and Foreign Trade*. New York: Cambridge University Press, 1987.

Thomson, Grahame, *et al.* (eds), *Managing the UK Economy: Current Controversies*. Cambridge, UK: Polity Press, 1987.

# 9    Greece

## A LESSON IN THE LOVE OF LIFE

In spite of structural unemployment, widespread poverty, political turmoil and an ambiguous position in the East versus West divide, the Greeks have a marvellous capacity to find stimulation in life itself. Greeks enjoy life and want to share their gusto with all who come in contact with them.

Business formalities such as professional titles, codes of behaviour, business taboos that are considered terribly boring. It is not uncommon for a Greek to ask early in an acquaintance what your income level is and what your family members do for a living. Greek business protocol is virtually non-existent.

The best attitude for a visitor is to leave behind all the usual rules of punctuality and tightness of the business world. Greeks will routinely arrive 30 minutes late for a meeting – in fact most people mentally adjust their expectations to take the delay into account.

At meals, men are encouraged to drink fairly heavily; work or an upcoming meeting is not a good enough alibi for not drinking. It is important to follow the lead of your host. The typical dinner will last long into the night, depending on the intensity of the conversation. Nothing is off-limits, with the possible exception of Cyprus and Turkey. Protocol only comes into play when an elderly person is present. In this case, it is advisable to use professional titles; for Greek culture is traditional, and male dominance is still very prevalent.

Most Greek men would consider it humiliating to help with the dishes or other housework. Men consider it a matter of personal honour to fulfil their obligations to their family. Honour is a key word here. 'Honour has no price, and joy is his who has it', goes the Greek proverb. Dignity, self-respect, independence and self-control are inherent to the Greek concept of *philotimo* (loving honour).

Yet with all the freedom, Greeks can be very conscious of proper conduct. Modesty, decency and propriety are paramount, particularly for women. The family's role in Greek society cannot be overstated: no member must ever bring shame or dishonour to the family, parental authority is not questioned, and there is general respect for elders.

The Greek family gives its members a place in national society and culture. A Greek earns recognition through the family, and depends on the family for reinforcement. The family is the basic economic unit of the country, responsible for the conversion and transmission of wealth to new generations.

But urbanization is beginning to affect Greek life. The formerly close-knit family is breaking down, and in the larger cities, family meetings are limited to major religious events such as weddings and funerals.

Greeks are warm and cordial in their personal relationships. Business is usually conducted over a cup of coffee. A wealth of good restaurants and places of entertainment makes it easy for business visitors to reciprocate the courtesies shown. But do not be deceived. Greek business persons are astute bargainers. Success in business dealings will depend on patience and quick judgement.

Some useful tips:

- Never refuse an invitation by a Greek business or government official.
- Do not contact a Greek at home or during his midday relaxation period.
- Avoid trying to do business at the dinner table.
- A hearty appetite is a sign of approval and is well received by your Greek host.
- Night entertainment is the norm. Be prepared to stay out past 'normal' hours.
- When selecting gifts for your host, avoid personal items such as ties, shirts, or cufflinks. Good gifts are coffee table books, desk sets, and table lighters.
- Share your positive impressions of the Greek countryside with your Greek partner.
- A slight upward nod of the head means 'no'. Also, a slight raising of the eyebrows is the non-verbal signal for 'no', as is a clicking of the tongue against the teeth.
- A Greek may smile not only when he is happy, but sometimes when angry.
- The Greeks have many non-verbal signals to ward off the 'evil eye', of which they have a strong superstition, such as a puff of breath through pursed lips.

Coffee houses are the focal point of leisure activity (mostly for men only). *Kouvenda*, conversation having no specific purpose other than the pleasure of vigorous speech, is a favourite pastime of Greek men in the coffee houses. Talk is loud, and verbal battles often erupt.

Upon introduction, men and women shake hands, as they do each time they see each other. One should not immediately launch into a discussion of business, but begin with polite inquiries as to the well-being of family, in the case of a good friend, or comments on the city or country in the case of a new acquaintance.

If invited to dinner, do not arrive early or more than 15 minutes late. Business is not discussed at dinner. A favourite topic of discussion is politics. Greeks love to argue for argument's sake and tend to philosophize problems away. Much like the French, they are intellectually curious.

Greeks are a very hospitable people and the visitor is received with much warmth. One should accept dinner invitations, as this is the Greek's main way of showing his liking and hospitality for the visitor. Gifts are not necessary, yet a small gift may be given after the first social meeting. Be careful not to admire and praise a specific object, for your host will very likely insist that you take it with you when you leave.

Greeks are expressive people. Raised voices, a variety of facial expressions and gestures are commonplace. A visitor to Greece who is unfamiliar with Greek culture may believe that a violent argument is under way when in fact two people are merely having a lively conversation.

*Philotimo* is a very important element of the Greek self-concept. It is a way of seeing oneself as a part of a system of group relatedness. The person who has *philotimo* is honest, respectful, and moral. Greeks believe this to be a value that knows no class boundaries. The greatest social disgrace is to lose *philotimo*.

The Greek Orthodox Church is the official church of Greece, and 98 per cent of the population belongs. The most important religious celebration in Greece is Easter; on Good Friday, churches are filled and places of entertainment closed. The influence of the church in the cities is declining, but remains strong in the countryside.

The Greek language is part of the Indo-European family of languages and the pure or formal form (*Katharevusa*) is used in literature, government work and for public signs. The popular or spoken form (*Dhimotiki*) incorporates words from other languages. Sometimes this causes problems for visitors. For example, the word for grocery store in *dhimotiki* is *bakaliko* but the sign says *pandopolion* (*Katherevusa*). The current trend favours the *dhimotiki* form. But language is not a major barrier to foreign business. Government officials and business people speak French or English.

Many multinational companies cover the Middle East from Athens, especially since the Persian Gulf War and civil unrest in that area. There are good airline connections with other major cities and substantial international banking facilities. Multilingual personnel are available, and living conditions for managers and their families are good. The foreign schools for French, Germans, Italians and Americans are considered high quality.

Many industrial firms are family-owned, for Greeks believe in owning and controlling their wealth rather than allowing assets to be controlled by others. They will borrow money from banks for business expansion rather than sell market shares to the public, they are generally unwilling to invest in enterprises outside the family business, and are reluctant to trust government with property or control over economic prospects. Because of these attitudes, the banking system has an unusually large role in industrial financing and the domestic capital markets are not well developed.

## HISTORY AND GOVERNMENT

Greece is the seat of Europe's oldest civilization. The nation's heritage is a reflection of values and wisdom of more than 3,000 years. A high degree of patriotism, cultural consciousness and ethnic cohesion is evident in modern Greece. The heritage of ancient Greece has been borrowed and applied throughout the Western world, and modern Greeks take great pride in this fact.

The word 'Greek' is derived from the Latin *graeci*, which was used to identify one Hellenic tribe and later applied to all Hellenes. For centuries, Greeks referred to themselves as Romans. It was only in the eighteenth century that the use of the term 'Hellenes' was revived.

Greek cultural life has felt the impact of its geographic location. Greeks often describe their country as the bridge between Western Europe, the Middle East and North Africa. A network of East-West and North-South land and water ways confirms this view.

Mountains constitute two-thirds of Greek territory, and communication was difficult before air travel. The seas around Greece have been its highways and influenced its destiny. It is bounded by the Ionian, Mediterranean and Aegean Seas. The seas pushed the Greeks outward while the mountains pushed them inward.

There are three groups of Greeks: city Greeks, seafaring Greeks, and rural Greeks (the most populous). The city Greeks, mainly in Athens, are self-confident, lively and very cosmopolitan. The seafarers are primarily fishermen and merchant seamen who feel at home in many ports of the world and speak many languages. They tend to look down on agricultural work. The Cretans are known for their bravery, independence of mind, and physical beauty. In Corfu, islanders are known for politeness and love of music.

Common beliefs about the sea dictate pride in being an islander. The rural Greek lives in the villages and towns of the mainland and large islands, where life is hard and traditional ways prevail. There is a dependence and closeness to the land.

Though Greece has had a history of military intervention in politics, the country was a monarchy until 1973. The last military junta took power in 1967. Its repressive, at times brutal, rule ended in 1974 when its disastrous intervention in Cyprus resulted in the Turkish invasion of the island. Today Greece is a parliamentary democracy. Its unicameral legislature elects the president. The 1975 constitution provided for a strong president modelled after the French system, though amendments to the constitution in 1985 stripped the president of most of this power.

Full-membership status for Greece in the European Community was granted in 1981, bringing opportunities as well as challenges. Businesses have had to deal with competition from the larger EC firms, and the government has had to liberalize its economic and commercial practices.

Parliamentary elections are held at least every four years, but may take place earlier if the president, in conjunction with the Council of the Republic, receives a vote of no-confidence.

Local government administration is divided between fifty-one prefectures, each headed by a prefect appointed by the Ministry of the Interior.

## ECONOMY

There is no elite landowning class, nor is there a class of landless peasants. Instead, the fragmentation of the land into smaller and smaller holdings has become a problem. Mechanization of agriculture and cooperative action – hence rural development – are inhibited.

There are several major social divisions in the urban context. The upper class consists of bankers, wealthy merchants, shipowners, industrialists, and some professionals and administrators. Among these are the aristocrats, who have had money for several generations, and the *nouveau riche*. A less prestigious level of the middle class comprises civil servants, shopkeepers, small merchants, and craftsmen. Most urban Greeks are middle class.

Government plays a big part in industry, and government intervention is likely to increase. A major disadvantage of dealing with the Greek government is the massive and slow-moving bureaucratic system, a full-scale streamlining of which may prove to be too much for one administration.

Greek export trade has been primarily agricultural (tobacco, dried fruit), although it is declining in importance. Major imports are capital goods. Greek shipping activities have long been significant in world trade. Earnings from tourism show great potential for growth.

Major areas of growing importance in the industrial category are textiles, iron, steel, aluminium, cement, and chemicals. Greece has large deposits of relatively untouched minerals which could be the key to growth and economic competitiveness in the future. Because of the high cost of fuel imports, Greece is seriously concentrating on the development and conservation of energy.

## BIBLIOGRAPHY

Constantelos, Demetrious J. and Efthymion, Constantine J. (eds), *Greece: Today and Tomorrow: Essays on Issues and Problems*. New York: Krikos, 1979.

Couloumbis, Theodore A., *The United States, Greece, and Turkey: The Troubled Triangle*. New York: Praeger, 1983.

Economist Intelligence Unit, *Country Profile: Greece*. London: The Unit, 1991.

Electra Press Publications, *The Greek Economy in Figures*. Athens: Electra Press Publications, Annual.

Freris, A., *The Greek Economy in the Twentieth Century*. New York: St Martin's Press, 1986.

Garland, Robert, *The Greek Way of Life: From Conception to Old Age*. Ithaca, New York: Cornell University Press, 1989.

Gianaris, Nicholas V., *Greece and Yugoslavia: An Economic Comparison*. New York: Praeger, 1984.

Mouzelis, Nicos P., *Modern Greece: Facets of Underdevelopment*. New York: Holmes and Meier, 1978.

Organization for Economic Cooperation and Development, *Economic Survey: Greece*. Paris: OECD, Annual.

Shinn, Rinn S. (ed.), *Greece: A Country Study/Foreign Area Studies* (3rd ed.). Washington DC: The American University, 1986.

Theodoracopoulos, Taki, *The Greek Upheaval: Kings, Demagogues, and Bayonets*. New Rochelle, NY: Caratzas, 1978.

# 10   Ireland

## THE WARMEST WELCOME

It is often observed that descendants of Irish immigrants, long removed from their homeland, continue to label themselves as Irish. The country's rich cultural heritage breeds a clannishness that serves them well at home and abroad. Irish expatriates in fact operate a 'Murphia' network to help each other in their basic needs, their careers and in maintaining their Irishness. In its own way, the Murphia is every bit as effective as Sicily's Mafia.

The Irish are a gregarious people. To an outsider, they seem in constant conversation with each other. The lack of an important fishing industry is attributed to the Irishman's aversion to staying away overnight on a fishing boat or for any other reason, since it would interfere with his need for conviviality.

The principal social institution in Ireland, after the church and the home, is the pub. Almost every Irishman will spend some part of each day in a pub. The Irish spend about 14 per cent of their disposable income on various forms of drink. The Danes, next in line, are a very poor second at 4 per cent.

The Republic of Ireland is the only English-speaking country that is Roman Catholic (95 per cent). Most families kneel together every evening to say the rosary at home, and people are in churches at all hours attending novenas, benedictions, making the stations of the cross or merely lighting a holy candle. The church is the only thing that comes before obligations to the family. Even with all this constant devotion, the Irish often express guilt for not doing enough for God.

When doing business in Ireland it is imperative to understand the history of the people – its effect on their attitudes, lifestyle and business style. Long years of hardship and suppression have made the Irish a hardworking people, quick-tempered, quick-witted and critical. The influence of Irish Catholicism is evident in all aspects of daily life and in the social structure. The strength of Catholicism fuelled the Irish desire for political independence from Great Britain, except in the predominantly Protestant North, which remains part of the United Kingdom.

Modern Irish people display an unmistakable link to their heritage as a nomadic people. The traditional art of storytelling through unaccompanied songs is the means for passing on the ancient legends and pre-Christian superstitions. Food is for sustenance (nothing fancy or heavily seasoned); clothing is plain, simple, and generally dark.

Blarney is another major art form and kissing the Blarney Stone is said to grant one the gift of persuasion. Hospitality is almost compulsive to the Irish: everyone is welcome, and a stranger who stops for directions will most likely find himself having tea or a meal, although the family may be destitute.

The Irish cherish the rain. When on rare occasions the rains stop for as much as two weeks at a time, the natives complain of drought and imminent bankruptcy. They believe water gives the island its richness and its character. This water is also translated by the skill of brewers and distillers into substances that promote the facility of talk.

Foreign personnel, except perhaps the British, are readily accepted by the community, which is open to other ways of life and business. The operative Celtic phrase is 'a hundred thousand welcomes', and the Irish live up to it, making the foreigner feel instantly welcome. The instantaneous friendliness can just as swiftly change to an unwelcoming or indifferent attitude. One should not take it personally if the doors which were so readily opened are suddenly shut. This is simply another manifestation of the country's temperament and quickly shifting moods.

Irish society is experiencing fundamental changes in attitudes on sex and women, bringing them closer to most European attitudes, but conservatism is still the norm. A constitutional amendment banning abortion was recently passed.

The family is still very important in Irish society and, although decreasing in size, families are large compared to other Western European countries. Relatives often live close to one another.

Owing to the social/sexual repression of the Roman Catholic Church, disturbing social trends are also evident in Irish life. Stressful marriages are perpetuated, and male chauvinism is prevalent. The combination of these factors has led to an alarming incidence of battered women and children. About 94 per cent of the population in the Irish Republic are Roman Catholic, and 4 per cent Protestant, principally Anglican (Church of England).

The population of the Republic of Ireland is approximately 3.5 million, about one-quarter of which is centred around Dublin. The standard of living is regarded as middle-ranking among European countries.

Irish life has been deeply affected by the conflict between the mostly Roman Catholic population of the Republic and the predominantly Protestant population of Northern Ireland. Most people in the Republic favour unification, but are opposed to violent means of achieving it.

People in the Republic speak both Irish and English, while English is the only official language in Northern Ireland, and even in the Republic, English is used for business and correspondence. The Irish language was revived after the founding of the Irish State in 1921, and remains important for the continuation of the ancient form of storytelling and unaccompanied singing.

Recently there has been a growth of Irish-speaking schools in urban areas. These schools were established and funded entirely by parents. There have also been attempts to revive the Irish language by transferring Irish speaking families to plots of land close to areas where Irish is not spoken.

## HISTORY AND GOVERNMENT

The presence of the Celts in Ireland can be traced to the fourth century. The Celts were a Gaelic-speaking people known as strong warriors. They were a tall, fair-skinned, race with reddish hair, and they spread thoughout the country in more than 100 tribes. The country was divided into five major kingdoms reflected in the four provinces today: Ulster (Northern Ireland), Munster, Connaught and North and South Leinster. Nationalism was unknown to the Irish of that day.

In 1170 the Normans arrived – the first fateful link with England. The Normans and the Anglo Saxons gradually became the English, who viewed the Irish as hostile, barbaric tribes, threateningly close and difficult to subdue. With Henry VIII and the Reformation in 1536, the conquest took on the viciousness of religious persecution.

The land that the English could not conquer they often took through legal procedure. An Irish landowner would be accused of treason, and forced to forfeit his land to the Crown. All the lands of Ulster were confiscated by Queen Elizabeth and redistributed among Scottish Presbyterians whose descendants are still living there, loyal to the British today.

The proud Irish chieftains wished to retaliate, the virtue of cooperation escaped them and they could rarely present a united front to the enemy. In 1641 they attacked Ulster, striving to reconquer the lands but managed only to massacre many Protestants. Many believe this is is the reason for the traditional Northern distrust of the South.

In 1649 Oliver Cromwell arrived, seeking revenge on the rebels. He eliminated the population of Wexford, women and children included, and swept the country, burning everything in his way until finally the Irish held only one-ninth of the country's land.

In 1690 the Irish rallied against William of Orange, today's hero of Northern Ireland, but they lost the Battle of Boyne on 12 July 1690, and became subject to the Penal Laws, which barred Catholics from all professions, took away their right to vote, hold office, teach or practise law. Catholic landowners could not leave land to one son, but had to subdivide it equally among them all, which decreased already uneconomical plots. The Irish were reduced to living as tenants to absentee landlords.

In 1780 things began looking up. The Parliament in Dublin ignored the Penal Laws, and England felt it might be safer if they brought the Irish Parliament to Westminster. England established the Act of Union, whereby Ireland became a part of Great Britain, no longer having its own governing body, but fully represented in British Parliament. In 1828 Catholic Daniel O'Connell was elected to Parliament in County Clare, and by 1829 had the Penal Laws revoked and Catholic emancipation proclaimed.

The Republic of Ireland was founded in 1921, with the signing of the Anglo-Irish treaty, giving dominion status within the British Commonwealth to twenty-six of Ireland's thirty-two counties. In 1948 the Republic of Ireland Act was passed, freeing the Irish Free State from any remaining constitutional ties to Great Britain.

Adversity aside, Ireland has maintained a close relationship with the United Kingdom. No passport is needed to travel between the countries and each can vote in the other's elections.

The Republic of Ireland is a parliamentary democracy. The Dail is the primary legislative body and is elected every five years by a system of proportional representation. The president has only limited power. Each president is elected to a seven-year term, generally by popular vote.

The Republic has been a member of the European Community since 1973. Neutral Ireland is the only EC country that is not a member of NATO.

## ECONOMY

Beginning in the 1950s, Ireland adopted a more outward-looking philosophy and shifted its concentration to export-oriented industry. The country enjoyed an economic revival in the 1960s, with continuous increases in employment and GNP growth; this revival was accomplished primarily by pursuing economic planning, emphasizing capital investment and realizing the economic benefits of foreign investment.

Today, Ireland's economy is one of the least prosperous in the EC. During the 1970s and 1980s, most of the growth has been in exports. The government has worked hard in the past two decades to promote growth. The electronics industry has been among the successful sectors, showing a growth in exports of 33 per cent, twice the per capita rate of Japan.

The government has actively encouraged foreign investment over these two decades. There are no minimum ownership requirements and no restrictions on foreigners purchasing land and property in cities and the larger towns.

In many ways, Ireland has become dependent on foreign companies, especially in the high technology, pharmaceuticals, and instrument engineering fields. Ireland is providing substantial investment incentives for foreign companies, including very low tax rates, non-repayable cash grants and 100 per cent training and research and development grants. The Irish Development Authority (IDA) is trying to encourage a shift to more capital-intensive operations for the foreign companies, because this will make them more reluctant to pull out of Ireland as soon as there is any change in the economy.

Emigration has resulted in a dramatic decrease in the population growth rate from 1981 to 1986. Presently estimated at about 30,000 to 40,000 per year, emigration largely occurs among 15-24-year-olds.

The resurgence of emigration, a recurring plague on the economy, is reaching a crisis level. It is not the unskilled or the unemployed who are leaving in the greatest numbers, but Ireland's best and brightest – recent graduates from the most highly respected universities.

For some, emigration is simply a matter of greater opportunities elsewhere. For others, however, the reason is sociological; their perception of Ireland is that of a country with ultra-conservative attitudes and without a sense of national pride, and they seek countries where attitudes are more open and there is a feeling of optimism.

## BIBLIOGRAPHY

Brown, Terrence, *Ireland: A Social and Cultural History, 1922 to the Present*. Ithaca, NY: Cornell University Press, 1981.

Cowie, David, *Ireland: The Land and the People*. Cranbury, NJ: A. S. Barnes and Co., Inc., 1976.

Economist Intelligence Unit, *Country Profile: Ireland*. London: The Unit, 1991.

Finnegan, Richard B., *Ireland, The Challenge of Conflict and Change*, Boulder, Colorado: Westview Press, 1983.

Finnegan, Richard B., *Ireland, Econonic Surveys, 1987-88*. OECD, 1989.

Foot, Paul, *Ireland: Why Britain Must Get Out*. London: Chatto & Windus, 1989.

Foster, Robert, *Modern Ireland, 1600–1972*. New York: Viking Penguin, 1988.

Organization for Economic Cooperation and Development, *Ireland*. Paris: OECD, 1990.

# 11 Italy

## MASTERS OF THE MISE-EN-SCÈNE

An Italian's true allegiance is not to his country, or to the law of which he is so suspicious, but to his family – still a quasi-sacred institution despite the many social changes Italy has undergone in recent decades. Without his family, the Italian has no source of honour, no social position, no identity.

Italian society, one of Europe's great patriarchies, revolves around the head of the family, the man who exercises full authority over its members. But of course life cannot be so simple. Italian women have traditionally been publicly 'subservient' to men, while in reality the 'Mama' functions as the real backbone of the family. With this in mind, Italy might better be called a cryptomatriarchy. It is not by chance that the most common expression in the language is 'Mamma mia!' and the next most common 'Madonna'. Italian men of all ages unashamedly display strong affection for their mothers.

Since the family network is the system, the Italian extends it to include his business colleagues and his friends, whom he calls cousins. Patrons and long-time friends become godparents and therefore members of the family. To succeed, however, one also needs to be clever. Subtle minor deceptions are considered commendable. Being the victim brings pity and contempt, as one who lacks the necessary contacts with which to beat the system.

Just as no Italian wants to be a fool, no Italian wants to admit that he is a 'nobody' without friends to do him favours. Therefore no one wants to pay full price for theatre or railway tickets, no one wants to pay full taxes, and no one wants to accept the listed price for a car or a suit. Only naive Italians and foreigners pay full price.

Survival in the official system, which is often considered hostile, requires a personal network. A successful person is said to have *raccomandazioni*, meaning good references with strong influence. Personal advancement is often directly related to the quality of one's *raccomandazioni'*.

Transparent deception, and flattery, which their countrymen understand for what it is, is practised by all Italians who feel a certain compulsion to make others feel privileged. The Milanese businessperson will offer a client an 'exceptional' deal, an opportunity not to be missed, an especially profitable venture at unheard of conditions, just 'for you'. Beware.

The Italian is a master at staging the right *mise-en-scène*, at making the right facial expressions, at using the right words, at wearing the right clothes to obtain the desired effect. New companies will put up impressive buildings for their lavishly decorated offices. Italians insist on wearing the smartest clothes, driving high-powered cars, and eating in the best restaurants, despite the financial burden.

Italians have long excelled where appearance is predominant. This explains their leadership in architecture, the world of fashion, the opera and the cinema. They have set standards for the world.

Since Italians attach such importance to appearance, it is not surprising that they should highly value physical beauty. Men are notorious for their preoccupation with their physical beauty, strength and virility.

In business as in life itself, Italians tend to be dominated by emotion rather than logic. An evening at the opera is not a chance to hear some interesting music, it is a sensual experience. But the ultimate dream of most Italians is less romantic: it is the conquest of security or *la sistemazione*, a secure if unglamorous job with a predictable career and a good pension at the end.

The way Italians address each other reflects the respect (*rispetto*) shown for the other person. *Rispetto* is based on the person's age, sex, and position in the family. A younger person shows deference to an elder, a woman shows respect for her husband, and a child for his or her parents. Wealth alone does not confer rank among the elite.

Perhaps the most formidable cultural obstacle for northern Europeans in Italy is the men's practice of walking arm-in-arm. Cross-cultural friendships have been dashed, and deals ruined, as Germanics recoiled at the Italian's friendly touch.

In a social setting, the eldest should be introduced first. Handshakes are used with men, women, friends not seen often, as well as with government officials. It is customary when visiting or coming to dinner to bring a wrapped box of chocolates or some flowers – an odd number – but not chrysanthemums, which are for bereavement.

If you are dining out, allow an Italian host to pay for the first meal. Following that meal, make an effort to reciprocate. While eating, Italians leave their hands on the table, and after each course, silverware is left on the plate. Dinner is a leisurely affair, lasting two or more hours. Guests should compliment their hosts on the meal.

Suitable discussion topics at the dinner table are politics, business, family affairs, local news, and sports such as soccer. Conversation is a favourite Italian activity. It is also a way of making the necessary impresssion on the others. Conversation and oratorical skills are considered important.

Reading facial expressions is a minor art form as practised by the Italians. Spoken words are often ignored, as they may contradict the accompanying expressions of the face. When negotiating, Italians watch each other's faces, looking for a decision or hesitation in the opponent's eyes. Indeed, strong eye contact may be used to stimulate a reaction from a foreign negotiator.

The ultimate decision-maker may sit in on virtually every meeting, but will reserve comment until the time of decision. Much of the input he offers is therefore through his observance of body and facial language.

With the exception of the northern businessperson, who can be cold, reserved and uncommunicative, Italians impress travellers with their enthusiasm and cheerfulness. Even those who serve seem to do it with pleasure.

Be prepared to engage in general conversation before beginning direct negotiations. An Italian must feel very comfortable with his negotiating conterpart before he can begin to make decisions. Don't be reticent about doing business over lunch; it is not uncommon to secure important business agreements at a lunch meeting.

A foreign business executive will be watched with much interest. Therefore be quite careful to follow proper protocol (e.g. wait for the host to initiate the topic of conversation). The fine art is to determine when exactly an Italian will be prepared to negotiate the 'nuts and bolts' of a deal.

In business customs, there is a clear division between Northern and Southern Italy. The North is conservative and formal, and the South is more casual. Personal contacts are as important in the North as in the South.

Some useful tips:

- Appropriate dress is a conservative suit. American 'power ties' (yellow or red) are considered in poor taste.
- Appointments for business and government visits should be scheduled in advance, and not in the early morning or immediately after lunch.
- While business cards are important, they are generally not exchanged until the first meeting is completed.
- Invitations and gifts may be used to lubricate the negotiation process.
- Correspondence with Italian firms should be in Italian. Do not assume your Italian counterpart speaks your language.

## HISTORY AND GOVERNMENT

Italy is a republic consisting of a boot-shaped peninsula 1,200 kilometres long, and two major islands, Sicily and Sardinia. Most of its boundaries are natural. To the north, Italy is separated from France, Switzerland, Austria and Yugoslavia by the Alps. It is bounded to the east by the Adriatic Sea and the west and south by the Mediterranean.

The proud people of Italy trace their roots to the Roman Empire, the greatest uniting force human civilization has ever known. Yet modern Italy has existed as a cohesive nation only since 1870. The traces of independence of Italy's former regions persist today, giving the country a wide variety of behavioural tones and colours. The Milanese of the north are as different from the Neopolitans of the south as the Swedes are from the Spanish.

Italy's government, the least stable of Europe, changed fifty times between the end of World War II and 1988, yet a sense of national purpose and a parallel system of self-governance keeps the economy and social services going. With the integration of European economies in post-1992 Europe, Italian institutions will be under pressure to conform to a higher European standard of predictability.

## ECONOMY

It is often said that Turin produces, Milan finances, and Rome consumes. Two other important cities, industrial centres as well as major ports, are Genoa and Naples. But in fact there are really two Italys: the North, which is highly industrialized and prosperous, and the South, known as the *Mezzogiorno*, which is agriculturally poor and underdeveloped. The *Problema del Mezzogiorno* is one of the government's most difficult and pressing tasks.

Most northern Italians think and work for individual profit. There are many small privately owned industrial and service based companies in this geographic area. In the South, most Italians secure employment by working for the state. The majority hold some type of governmental/ political job.

Although over 95 per cent of the Italians claim to be Roman Catholic, few actually practise their religion. Yet religion has always been a prime unifying factor; the Catholic church still plays a significant social and political role. Divorce is still not allowed, after many years of heated debate.

Private enterprise prevails, but the Italian government nevertheless plays an important role in the country's economy through state agencies which hold controlling interests in a number of large financial, commercial, and industrial enterprises. As in other European countries, state participation is very extensive in such areas as telecommunications, transportation (railways, Alitalia) and large shipping companies. Electricity, radio, and television systems are state-owned. In addition, the Italian government competes with private enterprise in several industrial sectors. The state has interests in mining, publishing, hotels and banks.

The majority of government interests are managed within four giant holding companies: IRI (Industrial Reconstruction Institute), EFIM (Manufacturing and Financial Holding Agency), and ENI (National Hydrocarbons Agency), which are supervised by the Ministry of State Holdings, and ENEL (Electric Power Agency) under the Ministry of Industry.

Most economic opportunities are open to foreigners, as Italy's foreign investment laws are among the most liberal in Europe. Repatriation of capital and related earnings without limit is guaranteed for 'productive' enterprises, i.e. those engaged in the production of goods and services requiring investment in capital equipment over an extended period.

## BIBLIOGRAPHY

Ciardelli, Quinto, *Evolution et Problèmes Structurels de l'Economie Italienne: Document Interne*. Brussels: Directorate-General for Economic and Financial Affairs, Commission of the European Communities, 1984.

Fraser, John, *Italy, Society in Crisis, Society in Transformation*. Boston: Routledge and Kegan Paul, 1981.

Grilli, Enzo R., *The Political Economy of Protection in Italy: Some Empirical Evidence*. Washington DC: World Bank, 1983.

Haycraft, John, *Italian Labyrinth: Italy in the 1980s*. New York: Penguin Books, 1987.

Kogan, Norman, *A Political History of Italy: The Postwar Years*. New York: Praeger, 1983.

Lange, Peter and Regini, Marino (eds), *State, Market and Social Regulation: New Perspectives on Italy*. Cambridge, New York: Cambridge Studies in Modern Political Economies, 1989.

Lange, Peter, and Sidney Tarrow (eds), *Italy in Transition: Conflict and Consensus*. London: Cass, 1980.

Organization for Economic Cooperation and Developement. *Italy*. Paris: OECD, 1990.

# 12    Luxembourg

## TINY BUT DETERMINED

Best of all, it is the national motto, *Mir woelle bleiwe wat mir sin* (We want to remain what we are), that reflects the independent character of the Luxembourg people. Despite the fact that the nation is split among people speaking French, German and Letzburgish, this small country is able to maintain a deep feeling of national pride. The population of 370,000 makes it the European Community's smallest member, but its aggressive financial institutions have ensured that it carries weight well beyond its tiny size.

Like most Europeans, Luxembourgers are reserved when first meeting strangers, but after the initial encounter they quickly become warm and friendly. The most common form of greeting is a handshake accompanied by an inquiry about one's health.

Personal appearance is highly regarded. For a Luxembourger, a first impression is rather difficult to change once it has been formed. Blue, grey, or black suits are appropriate attire for the business person. The younger generation is becoming more liberal, but society as a whole remains somewhat conservative.

The Luxembourgers rarely invite guests to their homes for business-related purposes, which are discussed in public places such as cafes or restaurants. If you are invited to dinner, it is appropriate to bring flowers for the hostess, and compliments on the dinner are always appreciated.

Catholicism is the most prominent religion in Luxembourg, accounting for 97 per cent of the population. The remaining 3 per cent is composed of Jews and Protestants. Catholic ceremonies and traditions are still adhered to, but the younger generation is becoming more secular.

The population is generally trilingual, with the majority also English-speaking. Letzburgish is used more as a spoken language in Luxembourg, newspapers are in French and German, and French is the official language of the civil service, parliament, and law. Students are taught in both French and German.

## HISTORY AND GOVERNMENT

The Grand Duchy of Luxembourg is a landlocked country bordering on France, Belgium and Germany. On a total land area of 999 square miles lives a population the size of an small European city, of which 26 per cent are immigrants from Italy and other Mediterranean countries. The general population is a mixture of nationalities – French, Belgian, and German – although the people are primarily of Germanic descent.

The northern and higher parts of the country are covered with forests and hilly terrain, a continuation of the Belgian Ardennes. The southern region is composed of farmland and woodlands.

Luxembourg is one of Europe's oldest and smallest independent countries, dating back to the tenth century, when Siegfried, Count of the Ardennes, constructed a castle at the site of present-day Luxembourg City. Several towns and villages grew up around the castle, and they required fortification and protection from enemies. Thus was formed the Luxembourg dynasty.

Luxembourg was ruled by the Austrian Habsburgs and then by the Dutch for the following nine centuries. It wasn't until the nineteenth century that Luxembourg was made an independent state and granted Grand Duchy status under the Vienna Peace Treaty of 1815. The treaty gave the Grand Duchy to King Willem I of Holland as compensation for his loss of land in Germany, but the King, also the Grand Duke of Luxembourg, granted the country its independence from the Netherlands. In 1867, the Treaty of London recognized Luxembourg as an independent nation and as a neutral country.

After being an occupied territory of Germany during both World Wars, Luxembourg abandoned its status of neutrality and became a charter member of the North Atlantic Treaty Organization.

Presently, Luxembourg is a constitutional grand duchy with the executive powers exercised by the Grand Duke and the Council of Government. The Council consists of nine members: a prime minister and eight other ministers. The prime minister is the leader of the political party, or coalition of parties, holding the most seats in parliament. The legislative power rests with the Chamber of Deputies, elected by the people of Luxembourg; and there is a second legislative body called the Council of State. The Grand Duke appoints the representatives to this body.

# ECONOMY

Luxembourg boasts a healthy and open economy, whose cornerstone is free enterprise. The government tries to encourage the well-being of private industry, but stops at direct interference. It has one of the world's highest gross national products (GNP) per capita at about $114,000. The unemployment rate is among the lowest in the world. After many years of continuous growth, the people of Luxembourg enjoy one of the highest standards of living among the European countries.

Even though it is small, in relation to its population Luxembourg is very highly industrialized. Part of its economic vitality rests upon the economic health of its major trading partners: Germany, Belgium, and France. Approximately 80 out of every 100 workers are engaged in foreign-trade-related activities. The major firms of Luxembourg are 95 per cent export oriented, yet the country must import over 90 per cent of its consumer goods. Recently there has been growth and diversification into the production of rubber, synthetic fibres, chemicals, plastics, glass and aluminium.

The country is a chief supporter of European economic unity and was a strong backer of the European Community's plan to eliminate trade barriers after 1992. In addition, Luxembourg belongs to the Belgium-Luxembourg Economic Union, which provides a common currency and monetary policy between the two nations. Trade practices are nearly identical as well, with manufacturers' agents and importers having offices in one or both cities. Luxembourg is also part of the Benelux economic organization, comprising Belgium, the Netherlands and Luxembourg.

Labour relations in Luxembourg have long been peaceful. Most workers are organized in unions connected to one of the major political parties, and labour disputes and issues are dealt with by representatives from the labour union, employers, and the government. Strikes only occur after a dispute has been submitted to the National Conciliation Office and all other mediation strategies have failed. Foreign firms are attracted to Luxembourg because of the peaceful, workable nature of its labour relations.

The steel industry remains the backbone of the Luxembourg economy, although the growth of new industries has lessened its importance. Luxembourg continues to flourish as an international banking centre and is ranked as the third largest banking centre in Europe. Lenient reserve requirements, and the Swiss style of banking, plus the absence of stamp duty on security transactions, have succeeded in guaranteeing Luxembourg banking prominence. Holding companies, which constitute a source of invisible earnings, have flourished, owing to favourable legislation.

## BIBLIOGRAPHY

Als, Georges, *Luxembourg: Historic, Geographic and Economic Profile* (original text in French). Luxembourg: Service Information et Presse, 1978.

Kurian, George Thomas, *Facts on File: National Profiles. The Benelux Countries.* New York: Facts on File Publications, 1989.

OECD, *Belgium-Luxembourg Economic Union.* Paris: Organization for Economic Cooperation and Development, Annual.

Price Waterhouse, *Information Guide: Luxembourg*, USA: Price Waterhouse, 1986.

Price Waterhouse, 'Luxembourg' (Developments in Individual Countries). *OECD Economic Outlook*, June 1988, p.127(1).

Price Waterhouse, 'Country Problems and Strategies' (Luxembourg and Italy's Economic Development), *OECD Observer*, vol. 143, Nov 1986, p.36.

# 13 The Netherlands

## EGALITARIAN ABOVE ALL

The Dutch sometimes seem a dour and austere people. Don't you believe it! Like many northern Europeans, they are only a bit wary. A heavy layer of formality governs their relations outside the family, making close business friendships slow to develop, especially with foreigners or others likely to be transient. But once sealed, the relationship will be highly regarded and long-lasting.

Only upon proper introduction would it be acceptable for strangers to communicate in personal ways, although this may vary from city to city. The Amsterdammer, for instance, is more chatty than the Haguener. Throughout the Netherlands, foreigners tend to be treated courteously as long as they do not call attention to themselves by being overbearing or insensitive.

Dutch business persons are a wordly, well-travelled lot, probably more cosmopolitan than most of their foreign partners. Thus they are quick to feel and resent any air of superiority or condescension on the part of foreign colleagues. One gaffe, frequently committed by foreigners, particularly annoys the Dutch: getting the name of their country wrong. It is the Netherlands, not Holland. The country comprises twelve provinces, including North Holland and South Holland. The other ten bristle at being called Hollanders – just as a Bavarian hates to be mistaken for a Prussian.

Almost half the country lies below sea level and is protected from flooding by dunes and a protective system of dykes. The saying 'God created the world but it was the Dutch who created Holland' has some validity.

Visiting business people are not usually entertained at home by the Dutch. If an invitation is extended, flowers for the hostess are in order, proper hours of arriving and leaving should be observed, and thank-you notes are appreciated.

After a dinner invitation out on the town, it is expected that offers be made to share the bill. The usual duel ensues betwen host and guest, with the host 'winning' the right to pay first time round. For the Dutch, such rituals add to the pleasure of the occasion, although the uninitiated foreigner may be confused.

For the occasional drinker, the strength of Dutch drink can be a shock. Be cautious of *jenever* (the Dutch equivalent of gin) *oude en jonge klare,* and *Bokma.* Drinking in bars is usually accompanied by appetizers called *warme hapjes,* or by various types of cheese.

Some tips to keep in mind:

- When invited to a Dutch home, bring a small gift of flowers or a bottle of good wine (which will most likely not be used that night, as special foods require special wine).
- Be punctual.
- Do not sit down or start eating until the hostess or your lady dinner companion does.
- Rise when women enter the room and wait until they are introduced and/or seated. Also rise when women excuse themselves from the table in restaurants.
- Rise for older people.
- Do not be familiar or tease the Dutch. A certain degree of formality is expected.
- Conversation is possibly as important to a Dutch person as the quality of the food.
- Gentlemen in Holland normally flank a woman on her left side while accompanying her.
- Do not extend too many compliments, and select modest adjectives when doing so. Hyperbole is frowned upon.
- When introducing people, introduce the younger, less socially esteemed or lower-ranking business associate to the elder, more socially esteemed or higher-ranking business person, rather than the other way around.
- In conversation, Dutch labourers are referred to as employees, not workers.
- Don't ask what political party a person voted for.

The Dutch tend to be particular about their dress and appearance, although they are less fashion-conscious than the Germans, Italians, or Spanish. Men's suits are far less body tailored than they are in other European countries. There is a strong influence on quality rather than quantity. Because of the climate, clothes are of heavier material than in many other European countries.

Holland's official language is Dutch, but English, French and German are generally spoken and understood by the international business community. To gain the confidence of the Dutch, or to put them at ease, it is of course better to speak their language. Actually, foreigners find it approachable, once the gutturals of the pronunciation are mastered. The old joke, that Dutch is a throat disease not a language, is an exaggeration; Dutch is closely related to German and to English.

A second language, Frisian, is the official language of the province of Friesland, and numerous dialects are spoken in the Netherlands.

The Dutch make wide use of the business lunch. The best time is from 12 to 2 p.m. The usual limit is one drink, most frequently cognac or sherry, before lunch and then wine, chosen carefully to complement the meal.

It is considered poor form to discuss business in the presence of non-professional women in restaurants or other social settings, including private homes. Increasingly, however, business discussions are taking place during golf or at social, business-related clubs. Business hours are strongly adhered to; working late is definitely not customary.

One of the decision-makers in the Netherlands, as in Germany, is the workers' council, a co-determination body for worker participation in management. The councils are advisory but often must give their consent before such decisions as transfer of control, organizational change, or entering or ending long-term commitments can be taken.

Dutch business ethics are strict, but the law exempts managers from personal accountability for mistakes. There is good job security and a strong sense of company loyalty.

In meeting people, the handshake is an all-pervasive custom, and this is repeated on subsequent meetings until people have become very familiar. The handshake is exchanged with men as well as women. Kissing a woman on the cheek is reserved for good friends and mutual liking.

Greetings are usually more formal than a casual 'Hi'. 'Good morning' or 'Good afternoon, Mr Jones' are more appropriate. A long period of formality usually elapses before the usage of first names. Family names are more commonly used. Government officials should be addressed by their proper titles. Formality also creates and maintains a distance between age and social groups.

The Dutch like to feel that sincerity and honesty are expressed through steady eye contact. Men tend to sink their hands into their pockets as a sign of comfort, but handshakes are never extended with the other hand in the pocket.

Table manners are also quite different in the Netherlands than elsewhere. Both hands should always be above the table, but the elbows should never rest on the table while eating. Food is hardly ever touched by the hand; even chicken bones are carefully picked off with knife and fork.

The Dutch enjoy talking about politics as seen from the outside,

European Community point of view. Sports, especially soccer, are comfortable subjects for conversation. In business situations, talk is usually confined to topics of general interest. Some Dutch are very sensitive, especially among the older generations, about Germans. Be careful about comparing them to Germans.

The Dutch are reluctant to offer personal information about themselves. Intimacy takes longer to achieve, but has a somewhat heavier weight attached to it, than in other European countries.

## HISTORY AND GOVERNMENT

The Netherlands is a constitutional monarchy located along the northern coastline of Europe, facing the British Isles across the North Sea. The country borders the Federal Republic of Germany to the east and Belgium to the south. Over the past few centuries, a great deal of territory has been added by reclamation from the sea and inner lakes.

The country is appropriately call The Netherlands, 'nether' meaning lower, because it almost entirely consists of flat lowlands. The highest point is only 1,070 feet, a point proudly considered a mountain by the Dutch. The main cities include Amsterdam, The Hague, Rotterdam and Utrecht.

The Netherlands was one of the world's main seafaring nations during the seventeenth century, but is now mainly a manufacturing nation. It formed part of the empire of Charles V in the Middle Ages and was later under French administrative control during the Napoleonic wars in the nineteenth century. French influence has persisted and is recognized in legal and some business aspects. Today's Dutch civil and commercial codes were originally based on the Napoleonic Code.

Former colonies of the Netherlands include Indonesia, parts of northern Brazil, Dutch Guyana, New Guinea, and a number of islands in the Caribbean. Today only the Netherlands Antilles remain.

The Netherlands is a politically stable, democratic nation under a constitutional monarch. It has been headed by queens for the past 100 years. The present queen is Beatrix of the House of Orange.

The government is composed of a coalition of numerous (splinter) parties. Parliament is divided into two houses, a First Chamber, or upper house, and a Second Chamber, or lower house. Political parties are proportionately represented in parliament. Legislation is passed after approval by both Chambers, then usually receives the royal assent.

About 36 per cent of the population are Roman Catholic and 30 per cent Protestant. The rest are largely nondenominational. Most of the Catholics live in the southern provinces of Brabant and Limburg. The royal family belongs to the Dutch Reformed Church. Although many political, social, and cultural activities are traditionally organized on religious bases, it can be fairly said that religion has very little influence on business or social relations.

## ECONOMY

The Dutch economy is based on private enterprise. The government has little direct ownership, but is heavily involved in the economy. State operations and social programmes amount to 70 per cent of the gross domestic product, representing the highest public spending as a portion of GDP among all European countries. The government makes its presence felt at all levels through regulation and permit requirement for almost all economic activities. Incentives are available to encourage investors to move out of traditional industrial areas such as *Randstad* (the areas surrounding the four major cities) and into the lesser developed eastern and northern parts of the country.

Industry employs almost 40 per cent of the work force in the areas of raw materials processing, oil refining, electronics, heavy metal and chemical products. Approximately 5 per cent are engaged in agriculture. Farms have become bigger, more mechanized and more efficient, and the country's agricultural products are successful export commodities. The rest of the work force is engaged in trading and the service industry.

## BIBLIOGRAPHY

Amsterdam-Rotterdam Bank NV, *Commerce and Industry in the Netherlands*. Amsterdam: AMRO Bank, 1984.

Centraal Bureau voor de Statistiek, *Statistical Yearbook of the Netherlands*. The Hague: Staatsuitgererij, Annual.

Dutt, Ashok K. and Costa, Frank J. (eds), *Public Planning in the Netherlands: Perspectives and Change Since the Second World War*. New York: Oxford University Press, 1985.

Koekkoek, K. A., *et al.* (eds), *On Protectionism in the Netherlands*. Washington DC: World Bank, 1981.

Kurian, George Thomas, *Facts on File: National Profiles. The Benelux Countries*. New York: Facts on File Publications, 1989.

Organization for Economic Cooperation and Development, *Netherlands, Economic Conditions 1945-*. Paris: OECD, Annual.

# 14 Norway

## THEY WARM UP SLOWLY

More because of geography than history, the Norwegian character is a blend of patience and fierce independence. A patriotic people, the Norwegians are proud of their bleak, far-off land. Fjords, the glaciated valleys filled by the sea, etch the entire coastline like a row of giant sawteeth. The struggle with the harsh and sometimes untamed environment has produced a tough, healthy and independent nation. Norwegians respect those who who are much like themselves – people with a sense of self-reliance and independence of mind.

At the outset of a business relationship, Norwegians may seem formal, stiff and unfriendly. But formality slowly dissipates as the relationship matures. True friendships become meaningful and sincere.

There is no complex protocol to observe in conducting business relationships, but as the Norwegians are health-conscious, cleanliness and neatness are always a must. Dress is conservative but informal. Norwegians are informal, and the phases of business are allowed to run their natural course, dependent on the personality of the business asssociates. Punctuality is a requirement for all business meetings. In fact, it is best to arrive a few minutes early.

Norwegians usually take the initiative in introducing themselves to strangers. At the first meeting, a handshake is standard practice and the grip should be firm.

A business contact is usually initiated by letter. Once contact has been made, appointments by telephone are appropriate. Upon first meeting, a name card should be respectfully presented, and a modest gift, such as alcohol or chocolates, is acceptable even at this time. The meeting should take place in the office and is often followed by a lunch at a good restaurant. The host is expected to pay for the lunch, but it is considered polite for the guest to offer to pay.

As Norwegians are hospitable, it is not uncommon for an out-of-town guest and spouse to be invited home soon after the first meeting. A formal banquet is usually not held between friends nor in honour of a business deal unless the relationship is a major part of the Norwegian's business. After a meal it is polite to thank the hostess by saying *Takk for maten.*

Toasting and speech-making are popular and much enjoyed parts of the dinner party. The host will begin by making a speech in honour of his guests and toast them all. The traditional method of toasting is still used in formal situations.

Rigid rules are rare in Norwegian conversation patterns. Topics of conversation are not fixed, although there are a few taboos – such as salary, social status, and employment.

About 95 per cent of the population belong to the Evangelical Lutheran Church, the state church of Norway, and there are about 150,000 members of religious communities outside the state church. However, most Norwegians go to church only on traditional holidays, such as Easter and Christmas, and for funerals and weddings. There is a popular and growing movement to separate the state and church.

## HISTORY AND GOVERNMENT

The typical Norwegian is of pure Nordic stock, tall, blond, with blue or grey eyes. The people are homogeneous, with traditional intermarriage largely limited to people of the other Scandinavian countries, Sweden and Denmark. In the south the people are generally shorter and of darker skin colour. They are thought to be descendants of slaves brought from the south of Europe by the Vikings.

A constitutional monarchy rules the country through the prime minister and the Storting (parliament) of 157 members in two houses.

Norway encompasses the western and northern areas of the Scandinavian peninsula and is surrounded by the sea on three sides. It is one of two NATO countries with common borders with the Soviet Union, the other being Turkey. From the north to the south, the country covers about 1,600 kilometres. The coastline is shielded from the open sea by a chain of islands, Skjaergard, stretching the entire length of the country.

Even though the Arctic Circle crosses through the mid-section of the country, the climate is warmed by the Gulf Stream, which keeps the harbours ice-free during the winter. The west coast has a mild winter, with temperatures around 1-3°C. But Norway's winters are long and dark, leaving a trace of gloom and depression in the national personality.

Norway is a sparsely populated country of a little more than 4 million people. Oslo, on the eastern shore, is the largest city and capital with 454,000 inhabitants. Other principal cities are Bergen, population 207,000, Trondheim, population 135,000, and Stavanger, population 92,000, all of which are on the west coast.

# ECONOMY

The Norwegian economy is in transition. The Ekofisk oil strike in 1970 brought a new prosperity, which, however, has slowed significantly since oil prices plunged in 1986. There has been a shift from the farming, fishing, and shipping industries to oil-related industries, building, commerce, manufacturing, and service jobs. Norway's oil and gas production account for about 10 per cent of the energy consumption of Western Europe. The expansion of modern industry is the most important factor in the national economy, primarily based on the country's inexpensive hydroelectric power.

The switch to an oil-based economy has brought its problems. The high wages paid by oil companies have distorted the wage systems throughout the country, forcing higher than usual wages in other sectors. The trend towards the support of the oil sector has also masked the fading of more traditional industries. The government encourages the traditional sector, at high-cost subsidies, because it is felt that employment generation has not come from the oil sector. Oil provides 38 per cent of exports, 21 per cent of tax revenues, and 19 per cent of gross domestic product. Norway is a member of the European Free Trade Association, and over 83 per cent of her trade is directed towards Western Europe. Norway rejected European Community membership in 1972, but may seek admission after 1992. Norway's largest trading partners are the United Kingdom and Sweden.

The development of the oil and gas fields in the North Sea is a major source of national income. Norwegian enterprises deliver an increasing share of goods, services, and technology, necessary for the development of the fields.

The Norwegian government places many restrictions on corporations operating in Norway. Although these restrictions are not always popular, they are upheld as the law. Honesty and integrity are important in the business community, it being considered inappropriate for a firm to try to find loopholes to circumvent the law. When a law is broken, there are no negotiations for a settlement; rather, the party is prosecuted and sentenced.

Although the oil industry is run primarily by the government, the Norwegian people have enjoyed only limited benefits from this wealth. Petrol, for example, is more expensive than elsewhere in Europe. Owing to an advanced programme of social benefits, taxes in Norway are high.

All transfers of foreign funds to Norway by non-residents for investment purposes are subject to approval by the Bank of Norway. As a general rule, all payments to foreign countries must be approved by the Bank of Norway.

## BIBLIOGRAPHY

Amundsen, Kirsten, *Norway, NATO, and the Forgotten Society Challenge.* Berkeley: University of California at Berkeley, 1981.

Ausland, John C., *Norway, Oil and Foreign Policy.* Boulder, Colorado: Westview Press, 1979.

Damman, Erik, *Revolution in the Affluent Society.* London: Heretic Books, 1984.

Derry, Thomas Kingston, *A History of Modern Norway, 1814–1972.* Oxford, Clarendon Press, 1973.

Derry, Thomas Kingston, *European Movement in Norway, Norway's Security and European Foreign Policy in the 1980s:* Report. Oslo: Universitetsforlaget; and Irvington-on-Hudson, New York: Columbia University Press, 1981.

Facts About Norway, *Aftenpasten*, Oslo: Chr. Schibsteds Forlag, 1970.

Jonassen, Christen T., *Value Systems and Personality in a Western Civilization: Norwegians in Europe and America.* Columbus: Ohio State University Press, 1983.

Kompass, *Register of Norwegian Industry and Commerce.* Stavanger and Oslo: Kompass-Norge 1982.

MacDonald, Greg, *The Nordic Countries and Multinational Enterprises: Employment Effects and Foreign Direct Investment.* Geneva: International Labour Office, 1989.

Nore, Petter, and Osmundsen, Terje, 'Norway – The Privileged Corner of Europe? Three Scenarios for Norway Towards the Year 2000', *Futures*, vol. 20, October 1988, p.568(10).

Nore, Petter and Osmundsen, Terje, 'The Future Belongs to Blondes' (Expansion of Norway's Public Sector), *The Economist*, vol. 306, 12 March 1988, p.47(1).

*Norway Information*, The Royal Ministry of Foreign Affairs, 1980.

OECD, *Norway*. Paris: Organization for Economic Cooperation and Development, Annual.

Poliszynski, Dag, *Negative and Positive Sides of Norwegian Life Style: An Empirical Assessment of Over-development.* Tokyo: United Nations University, 1980.

Price Waterhouse, *Information Guide: Norway.* New York: Price Waterhouse, 1988.

Rusoff, Denise, 'Norway', *Consumer Markets Abroad*, vol. 6, December 1987, p.169(4).

Spencer, Arthur, *The Norwegians: How they Live and Work.* New York: Praeger, 1975.

# 15  Portugal

## THE MELANCHOLY MISFITS

One of the most important traits to be aware of when dealing with the Portuguese is *saudade*, a feeling of nostalgia mixed with a melancholy acceptance of fate and a yearning for the past. Modern Portuguese are acutely aware of their nation's glorious achievements dating back to the fifteenth and sixteenth centuries – and equally aware of its poor-cousin status in the European Community (EC) today. The tension between the two ideas of Portugal sometimes produces a sense of unease, especially in the young.

Society is moving into the modern age, but in many ways still remains bound to the past. Networks of patronage spread beneath the surface, paralleling the laws and structures in place for the smooth and fair functioning of society. To some degree, of course, every society has its invisible networks, but in Portugal the links of kinship and influence are absolutely crucial to success. Young people on their way up must strive to be well-connected if they wish to further their own interests and standing.

Social relationships centre around who is related to whom, who knows whom and who owes a favour to whom. A foreigner doing business in Portugal must create such rapport and use new relationships as a stepping-stone for attaining goals.

The old-boy system is beginning to change, however, as the country integrates with the EC and people demand more from the system. It is striking to note how the quality of goods and services and the general smartness of shops have begun to improve in the past few years.

It is no longer a truism that the Portuguese would rather accept something that isn't quite perfect than argue over it. About 20 per cent of the population lives in the dynamic Lisbon area, typically Mediterranean, with its large squares, wide avenues, light-coloured buildings and palm trees, though on the Atlantic coast. The Lisboetos have an attitude of self-confident superiority. They consider themselves the focal point of the country and gladly accept the nickname *alfacinhas* or heart of the lettuce. Lisbon is truly the political, cultural and economic capital of Portugal.

Recent years have seen the rise of a new class, encompassing teachers, skilled technicians, mid-level business executives and a variety of other professions. As a result of this shift, the lower and upper classes are diminishing and being absorbed into the middle.

Yet Portugal on the whole does not yet display the dynamism of its Spanish neighbour, much less its competitors to the north in Europe. Punctuality, for example, is a low priority – so long as the fine points of etiquette are observed. An older person can arrive late for an appointment with a younger person, but not vice versa; a person of higher status can arrive later than a person in a lower position, but not the reverse; and a woman can keep a man waiting, but a true gentleman would not make a woman wait for him. To be safe on all counts, foreigners should simply be on time.

Portugal is one of Europe's oldest and newest countries in the sense that it was established many years ago and it has one of the youngest populations in Europe; approximately 23 per cent of the population is under 15, as compared to many other European countries, which have between 17 per cent and 19 per cent. Only 12 per cent are over 65.

Newcomers looking for business ventures in Portugal should expect a serious welcome. Meetings are generally formal and well organized. Business cards are exchanged upon meeting the other participants. When engaged in a private interview, it is acceptable to assume a friendly demeanour while always remembering to maintain a certain formality.

The Portuguese treat others in a dignified manner and expect to be treated the same by foreigners. Members of different social classes are careful to regard each other from the proper angle.

The Portuguese speak quietly and express their sense of humour with restraint. They are able to laugh at themselves, but it is usually inappropriate for foreigners to laugh at them. Their gestures as well as their tone of voice tend to be reserved. In general, it is best for a visitor to not be too 'physical', as they reserve this right for family and people they know well.

The Portuguese value tradition and are slow to accept change. It is therefore important to maintain a positive attitude with them and persist when attempting to introduce a new product or idea. After careful consideration and the passage of time, they will often change their way of thinking.

Above all, the Portuguese value personal contact, so it is imperative that firms visit their clients there, follow up on leads and perhaps hire a representative to work there. It is also important to have prompt follow-up to any sales, including servicing of equipment, even when distance makes this a hardship.

Although a clear class system is in place, a Portuguese of talent and dedication can rise from one social class to another. The class system is not based on birth alone; it also takes into account a person's formal education.

Although friendly and warm-hearted, the people rarely invite casual acquaintances into their private homes. Home entertainment is reserved for people who are trusted and considered as true friends.

But if you are invited to a Portuguese home, it is best to be punctual, dress conservatively and conduct yourself in a polite, restrained manner. Before entering your host's home, it is polite to wait outside until invited inside. Initially, casual chat should centre on your family, personal interests, positive aspects of Portugal and other safe subjects. The Portuguese do not appreciate a guest who is overly inquisitive or superficially friendly. Compliments can be made if they are stated with sincerity.

Upon departing, it is best to allow the host to open the door and let you out. A bouquet of flowers sent to the hostess the following day will be well-received.

The Portuguese are not excessive drinkers. Anyone who is seen drunk in public is likely to lose the respect of those around him or her. For a visitor, moderation is the byword.

## HISTORY AND GOVERNMENT

The country's sense of fatalism, almost disillusion, dates back about 500 years to a time when Portugal was one of the world's leading powers. Portugal virtually led the Western world with its technological advances in sailing and its expertise in navigation. Ships sailing under orders of Portuguese royalty carried the first Europeans to Africa south of the Sahara, to India and to the Far East. It is also believed that Portugal knew of the 'New World' six years before its discovery was claimed by Christopher Columbus sailing under the Spanish flag.

In 1578, Portugal was temporarily united with Spain and was compelled to conform to Spanish foreign policy, which ran contrary to its own. In 1640, Portugal regained its independence but it had already lost many of the previous alliances formed and territories held. The country never managed to regain her former position in the forefront of European development.

Most Portuguese, even if they are poorly educated, are aware of their dominance in history and their tremendous influence on the formation of the world in the fifteenth and sixteenth centuries. It is this knowledge that creates a sense of sadness, abandonment to fate, and nostalgia or *saudade* that seem to pervade the Portuguese character.

The Portuguese people as a whole seem to have a dogged sense of individuality with respect to other countries; they display a deep and passionate sense of patriotism. This desire to be recognized as a distinct nation, a distinct people, is best explained by a look at their history.

Portugal has seen many different peoples inhabiting its territory. The name Iberian Peninsula, of which Portugal constitutes only a small fraction, came from its first known inhabitants who were located in the southwestern region – the Iberians. Later, in the sixth century BC, the Celts crossed the Pyrenees and settled in the north.

The Romans conquered the peninsula in 200 BC and colonized it, dividing the entire expanse into three provinces. The area that makes up Portugal today they named Lusitania. They brought with them the Latin language, Roman law and Christianity.

In the beginning of the fifth century AD, several Germanic tribes defeated the Romans and became the undisputed rulers of the peninsula. At the beginning of the eighth century, they were pushed north by the Moslems from North Africa who occupied most of the peninsula for over 400 years.

The first king of Portugal, Alfonso I, fought hard against the Moors in an effort to regain the land to the south of what remained of the Kingdom of Portugal. He managed to recapture Lisbon in 1147 and thus was independence attained for the small nation. For another 100 years after Alfonso's death, his successors continued to battle the Moors until they had finally recaptured from them all the territory originally taken away. But it was not until 1263 that the Spaniards relinquished their last stronghold in the southern province of Algarve, thus giving Portugal its complete independence.

The Portuguese kingdom was then consolidated and began to grow and advance. A pact was negotiated with England in 1294 which was formally renewed in 1386 with the Treaty of Windsor. The Portuguese pride themselves on having the oldest existing bilateral defence agreement of the Western World.

The fifteenth and sixteenth centuries were marked by exploration and expansion of Portugal's knowledge of the world. Bartholomeu Diaz was the first to find his way to the Indian Ocean by rounding the Cape of Good Hope. Then, in 1498, Vasco de Gama reached India. This was truly a momentous voyage as he was in search of spices, a coveted commodity in those days used to hide the pungent flavour of meat. Two years later Cabral arrived on the shores of what is today known as Brazil. This age of exploration was followed by a sixty-year period of Spanish rule.

In an action to honour the Treaty of Windsor, Portugal took part in the struggle between France and England. When Napoleon invaded the Iberian Peninsula in an attempt to conquer the disobedient governments, the English, Spanish and Portuguese worked together and succeeded in pushing out the French army after seven years of fighting.

By the time that the nineteenth century was coming to a close, the coffers were empty; Portugal had spent all its money on rebuilding the economy and fighting wars. In 1910, the last monarch was removed from the throne and a constitutional assembly was formed. The next 15 years were marked by forty different governments and participation in World War I on the side of the Allies.

Immediately following the war, the government was seized by the military. In 1928, the position of Finance Minister went to an economics professor at the University of Coimbra, Antonio de Oliveira Salazar. He became premier in 1932 and for the next thirty-two years he maintained an authoritarian rule over the country.

When Salazar died in 1964, he was replaced by Marcelo Caetano. At first, it appeared that Caetano was going to be an innovative influence for Portugal, but he soon became more dictatorial than Salazar himself. A bloodless *coup d'état* was instigated on 25 April 1974 by the MFA (Armed Forces Movement) and General Spinola took control of the government. It was truly a revolution which ended in the drafting of a new constitution in 1976 to replace Salazar's 'new state' constitution of 1933. The new document leaned strongly toward Marxist principles and favoured a move toward socialism. Since then, however, privatization has been stressed, especially in the constitutional revision of 1982.

Since Caetano was otherthrown in 1974, Portugal has had sixteen governments. The situation appears to be improving, since, in the 1987 elections, the Social Democrats (PSD) won the first majority of the votes in Portugal's history.

## ECONOMY

Austerity measures imposed in 1984 by the Socialist-Social Democratic coalition government to combat the economic ills of the country, including high inflation, high unemployment and low economic growth, proved rather successful. Portugal has shown extraordinary improvement as a result of these measures, although the transformation has been painful.

Foreign investment is now being sought to improve technology and expand output, exports and employment. A favourable climate for foreign investment prevails, including low wage rates, an adaptable labour force, political stability, EC membership, geographic location and, of course, the recent liberalization of foreign investment regulations.

Unfortunately, there are several elements of the process that discourage business investment – the main one being the government bureaucracy, which must be patiently tolerated and which often turns away potential investors. Other disincentives include the inadequacy of the telecommunications and transportation systems within the country, and the lack of qualified management and poor organization across many industries.

Yet the economic situation is looking brighter all the time. Portugal entered the EC in 1986, and this has had a positive effect on the economy. One of the main beneficiaries of new investment is the agricultural sector, which has suffered from gross inefficiency and outdated methods of cultivation.

In the prosperous north lies Oporto, the nerve centre of the industrial region of Portugal and traditionally associated with the port-wine trade with Britain. Madeira, an island 675 miles off the southern coast, is the site of Portugal's third largest city, Funchal. The Azores, an archipelago which lies about 760 miles west of Lisbon, is also Portugese, with tourism, agriculture and cattle raising as its main industries.

About 75 per cent of the Portuguese population live in the rural areas, often without electricity, indoor plumbing or telephones. The population is expected to reach 10.9 million by 1995, though it declined between 1960 and 1970, due to a larger than usual outflow of residents to Portugal's colonies as well as to other European countries to participate as guest workers. However, owing to the granting of independence to the colonies in the 1970s and the return of many emigrant workers, Portugal has had to absorb nearly 1 million extra people. This has caused some problems, including an upward pressure on the employment rate.

Ethnically, Portugal is one of the most homogeneous countries in the world; there are no real ethnic, religious or linguistic conflicts. This could be a major factor contributing to its longevity – and its stagnation. About 99 per cent of the people are of Mediterranean stock.

The constitution guarantees freedom of religion, but approximately 95 per cent of the population are Roman Catholic. The number that attend church is rather high – 30 per cent as compared to 20 per cent in neighbouring Spain – but the church's influence is becoming less important.

## BIBLIOGRAPHY

Economist Intelligence Unit, *Country Profile: Portugal*. London: The Unit, Annual.

Livermore, H. V., *Portugal and Brazil*. Oxford University Press, 1963.

Myhill, Henry, *Portugal*. London: Faber & Faber Ltd, 1972.

'OECD Economic Surveys – Portugal'. Frost and Sullivan Political Risk Services, 10-1-87.

Maxwell, Kenneth, *Portugal-Ancient Country, Young Democracy*. Washington, DC: Wilson Center Press, 1989.

Robinson, Richard, *Contemporary Portugal*. Boston: Allen and Unwin, 1979.

# 16 Soviet Union

## ROULETTE ON A GRAND SCALE

In the early 1970s, a young Soviet manager in Moscow begged a Western colleague (or 'contact', to use the local terminology) to stop ringing him at home. 'One of my neighbours might answer the telephone. If he hears your accent, I've got real trouble. Befriending foreigners could ruin my career.' Today, this same Soviet manager rings his 'contact', now resident in London, long-distance from Moscow, and chats openly about the pros and cons of the historic political change shaking up his country; and he does not hesitate to criticize the Kremlin leadership.

In the space of a few eventful years, the Soviet Union has gone from one of the world's most stable totalitarian states to a nation in the throes of great change – and thus one of the most fascinating and unpredictable. Democratic forces are rising up to demand a higher standard of living and a multiparty political structure. Several of the fifteen 'republics' that make up the Soviet federation are demanding independence from Moscow. The loss of iron control at the top will mean the country must seek a new equilibrium of its own.

Once a market hostile to Western business concepts, the Soviets now seem ready to experiment with free-enterprise capitalism on a large scale. Having no memory of free choice in economic or political matters, the Soviet people face an unknown future. The Moscow manager now tells his friend in London, 'We don't know how to make it work. Come and help us do business'.

Western business executives are surprised at the speed with which some Soviets have embraced the principles of entrepreneurship and profitability. The acceptance of the new Western ideals of self-reliance and individuality is far from generalized, however. A collectivist mentality predates the Communist revolution of 1917, and provides the basic continuity that seems to survive all political change.

The turmoil has made the Soviet people more open to foreign contact than at any time since the late 1920s. Sometimes the Soviets seem overly eager. As a travelling Soviet academic said to a British friend in London in 1990: 'I want to see as much as I can on this trip. We don't know how long our freedom of movement will last'.

The politics may change, the rhetoric may die down, but the Russian character stays the same. There is a burning curiosity about the West, and a natural affinity with certain of the European nationalities – France in particular. French culture was always pre-eminent under the tsars. In fact the nobility preferred the French language to Russian.

Other constants that outlive political fashions include the *Ruskaya dusha* – that capacity for suffering, introspection, deep faith and emotionalism known as, for want of a better term, the Russian soul. The Russian people harbour a warmth and compassion quite in contrast to the sterile political ideology that has coloured relations with the West, both political and commercial.

At first, Soviets, especially Muscovites, may appear stiff, dull, and even cold. Facial expressions can appear blank and uninterested. Smiles and laughter are rare in public, except between people who are very close. Yet among friends, the Soviets quickly go beyond the range of public emotion usually practised in Western Europe. Physical contact is common in public. Hand-holding or walking arm-in-arm, even among members of the same sex, is normal. Friends hug each other warmly when they meet. Men kiss each other on both cheeks when they meet after a period of separation. A stiff and formal behaviour during work and in public hides a warm and gregarious individual within. In private, most Soviets will become very informal, hospitable, and fun-loving.

The visitor is advised to refrain from physical contact, however, unless it is initiated by the Soviet acquaintance. Among strangers, space is treated with respect. As relations warm up and mutual trust grows, the space will narrow. If actual friendship develops, close, physical contact will become natural, at least for the Soviets. It must be acknowledged, however, that true friendship in the business environment is rare.

When speaking to foreigners in Russian, Soviets typically employ *gospodin*, *gospozha* or *tovarisch* (comrade) as a form of address. This is a somewhat stilted form of high respect reserved for foreigners, which also implies distance. In formal situations, Soviets will refer to one another by last, or family name.

In other situations, the name game becomes more complicated. Soviets who have made even temporary acquaintance will generally ask one another for their *imya* (first name) and *ochestvo* (patronymic, or father's first name). The patronymic is usually formed by adding *ovich*, for men, and *ovna*, for women, to the father's first name. This is a standard way of addressing a person informally. Soviets treat their foreign acquaintances in much the same manner, and no matter how clunky a foreign patronymic might sound in Russian ('Hilary Nigelovich', for example) they may be offended if it is not accepted as a token admission of familiarity. The first name is traditionally reserved for close friends and family, although such rules are easing. Indeed, among Soviets who deal frequently with foreigners, most of the above is ignored, and forms of address go from 'Mister Smith' to 'John' in a matter of hours.

For the Westerner conducting business in the Soviet Union, anything faddish is to be avoided, in clothing as well as personal grooming. The Soviets are not intolerant, but they have an image of how a serious-minded adult engaged in business matters should look. Soviet officials enjoy special privileges and dress much as business people in the West, usually in a conservative suit. Away from the office or negotiating table, one may dress casually. Any social activity that includes meals, however, demands a more formal attire.

Women in the Soviet Union are often employed in menial jobs, but many hold responsible positions in business and government. A female Soviet official or executive should of course be treated as an equal. Surprisingly, chivalry is very much in order, and the Soviet woman enjoys gentlemanly gestures. For example, it is acceptable to light her cigarette. A handshake is offered by, not to, the woman.

Soviet officials are famous for being generous hosts. Dinners are long and elaborate affairs and toasts are frequently offered to seal business relationships and friendships. The hosts start this ritual and the guests are expected to reply. An art form unto itself, the toast is often lengthy and witty. In formal settings, toasts are made while standing, while other members of the party remain seated. The actual drinking requires that everybody rise.

Every social occasion seems to be accompanied by a bottle of vodka and sometimes champagne. Soviets are prodigious drinkers, and attempts to refrain from drinking are next to impossible. Although it is acceptable to overindulge, one is expected to keep a sense of propriety. An obnoxious drunk is highly offensive.

The basis of certain good Russian manners is mutual respect and a sense of wishing to be helpful to each other. This is coupled with a rather puritan public morality – a law-and-order outlook – although the greater freedoms now allowed by *glasnost* and *perestroika* have led to less rigid behaviour on the streets. Undue personal noise or anything ostentatious is frowned upon.

The Soviets believe in showing respect to any citizen who has earned a superior position. They treat each other with the courtesies accorded to age, rank, and experience, and they expect similar treatment from their foreign visitors. Small gestures as to who sits first, is greeted first, or perhaps is even bowed to first are important.

The following social customs should be honoured in order to reduce offence or misunderstanding:

- A handshake is the proper form of greeting.
- Soviet citizens are mindful of their nation's greatness and prestige.

- Atheism is not the state creed it once was; religious freedom is spreading.
- The most popular medium of exchange and a recognizable means of obtaining favours is a bottle of vodka. Good brands are difficult to obtain in stores, so it becomes a welcome gift for officials or business contacts.
- Women appreciate receiving Western cosmetics, which are unavailable locally.
- Yellow flowers given to a woman can be read as a symbol of grievance or separation.
- Avoid referring to the Soviet Union as Russia.
- Littering is strictly forbidden and violators are sometimes arrested.
- Do not bring into the country an excessive quantity of jeans, rock records, or other pop culture items that might be thought destined for the black market.
- Small souvenirs are considered good social etiquette: chocolates, a lighter, a bottle of French cognac, ballpoint pens – nothing too expensive.

Russian is the primary official language of the Soviet Union, and personal advancement within the system requires mastery of Russian. Over 75 per cent of the Soviet population have one of the Slavic tongues as their native language. Although the ethnic Russian segment of the Soviet population has been declining, the portion of the population that considers Russian its native language has been increasing. Some of the other 112 official languages are Armenian, Azerbaijani, Byelorussian, Georgian, Tatar, and Ukrainian. English is the most common foreign language taught in school, but is not widely spoken.

## THE ECONOMY

The current reforms that are reshaping Soviet society were prompted by the country's long-simmering economic crisis, publicly recognized by Mikhail Gorbachev only in 1986. The Soviet gross national product has never been accurately measured, but Soviet economists knew in the 1970s that the GNP gap with Western industrialized countries was widening. Virtually no economic growth has been achieved for the past 20 years. The declining standard of living was attributed to the country's 'command economy' system, and reforms were proposed. The process of recovery is expected to take at least 10 years, and Soviet economists warn that no improvement should be expected until about 1995.

The strengths of the economy are its relatively abundant raw materials such as oil, natural gas, coal, timber and gold. The weaknesses are in the full range of manufacturing industries. The acknowledgement of a crisis has led to open courting of Western companies to invest in joint ventures with Soviet partners. The objective is to achieve a steady transfer of technology from the West, which in turn might create the foundations for internal development.

The Soviet economy is in the midst of radical change. Some factories now have control over a greater percentage of their output and are finding the freedom to be a mixed blessing. Unreliability of supplies and poor-quality workmanship now have a direct impact on plant performance. The concept of accountability makes management uncomfortable.

The private sector of the Soviet economy is small but growing. In previous years, it was only in agriculture (where private production on small plots accounted for 25 per cent of the total gross output) that private enterprise played a significant role. But the co-op movement is the newest fast track for would-be entrepreneurs. The co-ops are privately owned and profit-oriented, and are supposed to introduce new vitality into the Soviet economy.

The basic instrument of control for seventy years has been The Plan. The current plan has some very aggressive goals, with *perestroika, glasnost* and democratization being the themes for economic as well as social development. The main objective of the Party's economic strategy is a steady rise in the people's well-being. Since the advent of *glasnost*, there has been a definite increase in freedom of speech; but in spite of efforts through *perestroika*, the Soviet people have seen a decline in goods available.

Economic reform has been the subject of heated debate for several years, and now is beginning to find its way towards a market-orientated system. How smooth the transition will be is an open question. The Soviet people have been used to cheap prices for the goods that were available. Now, what is available is of higher quality, but also higher in price. Although the economy is actually worse than before *perestroika*, the long struggle to reform such stagnant conditions may well bear fruit through the determined efforts of the Soviet government and people.

The Communist Party of the Soviet Union plays an integral, though changing role, in the operation of the Soviet government and economy, and radical reformers complain that the leadership and administration of the Soviet economy are still connected closely to the Communist Party. Although there is a new realization that the problems stem from too much centralization, it may take a while for the long-entrenched Soviet bureaucracy to give way to the tide of change.

Elections are now commonplace, with multiple candidates for most positions. Not only do the voters have a choice among candidates, but they have the option to vote against a candidate if they wish. In this way, some top Communist officials have lost their office, even if no one was running against them.

Until recently, the Ministry of Foreign Trade was the focal point for business conducted with the Soviet Union, but the reforms of *perestroika* abolished the Ministry in January 1988. Most individual firms are free to conduct their own negotiations, with some sensitive areas such as national security issues being overseen by one specialized trade ministry (where there were once three ministries to deal with).

Although a free-market system without central planning is in preparation, for the moment the Central Planning Board draws up the foreign trade plans. The Council of Ministers is the highest government agency responsible for determining national economic policy, which includes development of foreign trade, but the State Planning Committee does the actual planning of volume of trade, composition of exports and imports, and the geographical distribution of trade.

However, the reform-minded Soviet leadership is giving Soviet production ministries and some more individual enterprises the right to deal directly with foreigners, thus breaking monopoly control over imports and exports. In addition, the ministries and enterprises are able to engage in joint ventures with capitalist countries. The recent joint venture law allows over 50 per cent ownership and repatriation of profits, tax incentives for reinvestment, the ability to open operations in third countries, and protection against expropriation. Joint venture legislation is in a constant state of change, however, and must be checked periodically.

The Soviet market cannot be approached half-heartedly. Enormous perseverance and hard work on the part of a Western firm are required. Organizations that have been successful have developed long-range strategies. It usually takes years for a newcomer to gain a foothold.

Foreign business representatives are able to function more easily than before. A few years ago, Moscow had no comprehensive telephone directory and no detailed street maps. The foreign community relied on a map compiled by the CIA and published by a Soviet emigre press, which was available only in New York, Washington and a few other major cities in the West. Today, in a joint venture with Maul Belser, a publisher in Nuremberg, Germany, a Moscow yearbook called *All Moscow* is being produced for the business community. It contains maps, addresses and telephone numbers for every imaginable product and service offered in the city. But Moscow remains a hardship post by any standard.

One special problem that takes some getting used to is the Soviet attitude towards time. As in most of Asia, the idea of time is far less rigid than in the West. The Soviets are approximate in their appointments, as if to say, 'There's no reason to hurry. Relax'. They particularly dislike the quick tempo of Western business and the attitude that time is money.

They are happy to devote far more time and manpower to negotiations, and will use the slower tempo to good advantage. As a Russian proverb says: 'If you travel for a day, take bread for a week'.

The Soviets are renowned for their negotiating style. They will stall for time if they think they can get a better deal, and are famous for unnerving Western negotiators by continuously delaying and haggling. The Western negotiator can try the same tactics, but often must eventually acknowledge that negotiations must be brought to an end and the losses written off.

There are differing opinions on the wisdom of having Russian-speaking members on the Western negotiation team. On the negative side, the Soviets lose a subtle psychological advantage of being able to use Russian among themselves for personal deliberations. They will be on their guard in the presence of a Russian-speaking Westerner, and they may even be suspicious if he or she happens to be an emigre or second-generation Russian. On the positive side, a Russian-speaking team member can bridge communication problems and help build inter-personal ties. Since English and German are largely reserved for technical discussions, the Soviets feel more comfortable using Russian to discuss non-business matters.

It is a good idea to have on hand a large supply of business cards. The university degree of the Western business person should be included, and all cards should be printed in Cyrillic. At negotiations where large numbers of Soviet officials are present, be sure to hand out to everyone a card.

English is the most common foreign language spoken by Soviet foreign trade officials. Many also speak German.

## HISTORY

The Soviet character is marked by a succession of invasions, from the Tartars, Khazakhs, Varangians, Swedes, Poles, French, and, most recently, the Germans. Further, the Soviet Union has been oppressed by its own rulers. Such a bloody history helps explain why the Soviet people seem so passionately possessive of their land, so distrustful of foreigners, so submissive to authoritarian rule. Their patriotism is probably the country's most powerful unifying force.

The current drift towards an open society and a market economy is sure to be a path strewn with obstacles. The Soviets are not taught to be individualistic; they tend to see themselves as part of the collective, and feel comfortable when attached to a group.

The idea of the collective runs deeply through the Russian soul. The conquest of forest lands by peasants over 1,000 years ago was a group endeavour. Under the tsars, planting and harvesting were organized on a communal basis. In the Orthodox Church, confession was a public ritual symbolizing the sinner's return to the community of worshipers, and the individual learned to be subordinate and merge himself into the common fold. With this background, any vision of a Western-style Soviet Union in the twenty-first century seems highly unlikely.

The Union of Soviet Socialist Republics was created by the Russian Revolution of 1917. The ideals of Communism as a panacea created a sense of euphoria in the country at first, but in the 1930s a centralized and paranoid party apparatus under Joseph Stalin transformed the country into a totalitarian state from which it is only now emerging. The legacy of suffering under Stalin marks contemporary society, more so because *glasnost* has allowed open discussion of mass murder and oppression. Nearly every Soviet family has a relative or neighbour who lost loved ones in Stalin's terror.

Today it is the world's largest country in geographical terms, occupying more than 8.6 million square miles, almost one-third of the total land mass of Europe and Asia and one-sixth of the world's surface. It is significant that only about 25 per cent of the Soviet Union is in Europe; the rest sprawls across Asia. Owing to the vastness of the country, climatic conditions vary from subarctic to subtropical.

The length and severity of the winter rules out at least half the country's land in the north and east for agricultural purposes. Only in four small areas – along the Baltic and Black Seas and near Afghanistan and China – are there long, warm growing seasons. Much of the Soviet Union's northern reaches comprises a belt of permafrost.

The Soviet Union is a country of enormous ethnic and cultural variety. More than 120 distinct and separate nationalities inhabit the Soviet Union, speaking over 130 different languages. People of Slavic origin, principally Russians, Ukrainians, and Byelorussians, account for 72 per cent of the total population, and Russians represent only 52 per cent. By the year 2000, the Russian population will be in the minority.

The various ethnic and national groups are now beginning to voice long-held resentments. Independence movements and open condemnation of Moscow rule are features of the new era of free expression.

Freedom of worship is a right guaranteed by the Soviet Constitution, as is the right to anti-religious propaganda. There are over 50 million members of the Russian Orthodox Church. Islam is well entrenched in the southeastern regions of the Soviet Union. Judaism, Roman Catholicism, and Protestantism are all represented, primarily in the western regions. The Soviet Union's Jewish population is the third largest in the world.

The question hanging over the future of the Soviet Union today is one of leadership. Can the current leaders make their reforms pay off rapidly enough to calm internal dissent and to appease the various independence movements among the republics of the federation? Many observers believe that recovery by the mid-1990s is optimistic. Worsening morale among the population may in turn threaten the stability of the Kremlin reformers. Who would take their place? It is not clear.

## BIBLIOGRAPHY

Aganbegyan, Abel, *Moving the Mountain, Inside the Perestroika Revolution.* London: Transworld Publishers Ltd, 1989.

Aganbegyan, Abel, *Inside Perestroika.* New York: Harper and Row, 1989.

Asland, Anders, *Gorbachev's Struggle for Economic Reform.* Ithaca, NY: Cornell University Press, 1989.

Cohen, Stephen F. and Rabi, Alexander *et al.* (eds), *The Soviet Union Since Stalin.* Bloomington: Indiana University Press, 1980.

Cohen, Stephen F., *Voices of Glasnost: Conversations With Gorbachev's Reformers.* New York: Norton, 1989.

Cooper, Leo, *The Political Economy of Soviet Military Power.* New York: St Martin's Press, 1989.

Dmytryshyn, Basil, *USSR: A Concise History.* New York: Scribner, 1971.

Doder, Dusko, *Gorbachev: Heretic in the Kremlin.* New York: Viking 1990.

Ellman, Michael, *The USSR in the 1990's: Struling Out of Stagnation.* New York: Economist Intelligence Unit, 1989.

Eyal, Jonathan (ed), *The Warsaw Pact and the Balkans: Moscow's Southern Flank.* New York: St Martin's Press, 1989.

Gray, Francine, *Soviet Woman.* New York: Doubleday, 1990.

Gregory, Paul and Stuart, Robert, *Soviet Economic Structure and Performance.* New York: Harper and Row, 1990.

Gruzinov, Vladimir Petrovich, *The USSR's Management of Foreign Trade.* White Plains, NY: M. E. Shore, 1979.

Kaplan, Stephen S. and Tatu, Michael *et al.*, *Diplomacy of Power: Soviet Armed Forces as a Political Instrument.* Washington DC: Brookings Institution, 1981.

Medishsa, Vadim, *The Soviet Union.* Englewood Cliffs, NJ: Prentice-Hall, 1981.

Nove, Alec, *Glasnost in Action.* Boston: Unwin and Hyman, 1989.

Rees, David, *Peaceful Coexistance: A Study in Soviet Doctrine.* Washington, DC: International Security Council, 1989.

Ripp, Victor, *Pizza in Pushkin Square: What They Think of Us In The USSR.* New York: Simon and Schuster, 1990.

Schweitzer, Glenn E, *Techno-Diplomacy: US-Soviet Confrontations in Science and Technology.* New York: Plenum Press, 1989.

Shirley, Eugene B. and Rowe, Michael (eds), *Candle in the Wind: Religion in the Soviet Union*. Washington, DC: Ethics and Public Policy Center, 1989.

Shmelev, Nikolai and Popov, Vladimir, *The Turning Point: Revitalizing the Soviet Economy*. New York: Doubleday, 1989.

Taubman, William, *Moscow Spring*. New York: Summit Books, 1989.

Treadgold, Donald W, *Twentieth Century Russia*. Boulder, CO: Westview Press, 1990.

Winiecki, Jan, *The Distorted World of Soviet-Type Economies*. Pittsburgh, PA: University of Pittsburgh Press, 1988.

Wolf, Thomas A, *Foreign Trade in the Centrally Planned Economy*. New York: Harwood Academic Publishers, 1988.

# 17   Spain

## STILL A MAN'S WORLD

A newly arrived foreign business person must be prepared to be completely submerged into the Spanish system. And it will be a cold shower of cultural shocks and barriers. The value of being *bien educado* in the broadest sense is of primary importance, and success in business and in social settings will depend on one's ability to divine the proper protocol and operate confidently within it.

Most importantly, class distinctions are alive and well in Spain, and the monarchy holds the highest place of honour of all. (Obviously, conversation about the monarchy should range from positive to ecstatic.)

The Spanish people take an enormous delight in life, as witnessed by their many festivities and highly developed worlds of music, art and dance. This exuberant streak can be traced back five centuries, when Spain was a world power. Spanish wealth financed the exploration of North and South America.

Today almost half the Western hemisphere speaks Spanish. Spaniards made strides in music, art, literature, science, religion, and politics in an age when other countries were emerging from their Dark Ages. Memories of this grand past help explain the exaggerated sense of pride displayed by the Spanish today.

The country's history has been scarred, however, by foreign occupation. Roman ruins can be found outside Madrid, Moorish castles are abundant throughout the south of Spain, and nearly every country in Western Europe has contributed to the country's ethnic heritage.

Perhaps one of the more difficult issues for a foreign visitor to understand is the value of *enchufado*, being well-connected. Personal ties often serve as the critical lubricant for getting a job done. Control of Spain is estimated to be in the hands of about 200 leading families. To have a connection with one of these families almost guarantees success. There are eight large family-owned banks which control much of the economy. Good rapport with the key players can make the difference for a foreign investor as well as for a Spaniard.

To a Spaniard, the circumstances of a person's life are what give it meaning. As they like to put it: 'Yo soy yo y mis circumstancias' (I am myself and my circumstances). The Spaniard is fiercely independent while at the same time friendly and arrogant, a mixture of traits that leaves some foreigners confused.

Guests are usually treated with the utmost courtesy. Foreigners will often be told: 'Esta es su casa' (This is your house). A foreign guest will be made to feel at home as long as he observes the traditions of the country.

Sex roles in Spain are sharply delineated. The male is expected to be aggressive and dominant; the woman is taught to be passive and accepting. Although this division is becoming less rigorous, men still provide food and shelter, and protect the honour of the women in the family. Generally speaking, women are expected to devote their efforts to the home and child-rearing. These roles are further highlighted by the traditions of *machismo*, or *hombria*, which place an exaggerated emphasis on masculinity and ways of proving it.

The concept of honour is at the core of masculinity and is deemed superior to values such as efficiency, organization or business acumen. The visitor must be careful not to offend the Spanish sense of honour on either the personal or the business level.

Post-Franco Spain has experienced dramatic changes. Spain's entry into the European Community (EC) in 1986 has intensified the work ethic and quickened the pace of activity. Midday siestas, long lunches and frequent coffee breaks can be deceptive. In fact, Spanish workers and professionals are dedicated and dependable.

Business executives sometimes strive to give the impression that they are not working hard. This attitude survives an earlier time when it was not considered genteel to do physical work, or much work at all.

The Spanish have achieved something few other societies are capable of: a healthy balance between hard work and relaxation. A foreign visitor should be prepared to mix these two elements.

The Spanish tend to be physical. Men who are close friends often give each other an *abrazo* (embrace). When meeting a woman for the first time, the usual greeting is a handshake. Women and men who are close friends greet with a kiss on each cheek. If a Spanish friend introduces you to a close female friend, you are expected to perform the traditional peck on each cheek. This custom is not, however, extended to the business environment, where the handshake is the most common introduction.

Do not be surprised to find that by the second meeting your Spanish colleague grabs your arm in a friendly gesture. The Spanish, as some other southern Europeans, are accustomed to linking arms when walking along the street. They use the friendly touch as a means of emphasizing a point. Northern Europeans often cause offence by resisting.

Some behavioural tips:

- The Spanish enjoy vigorous discussion that often develops into combative argument.
- A Spaniard will always insist that his guest walk through a door before him.
- A Spanish citizen will insist on paying the bill at restaurants. The guest should insist on paying next time around.
- The Spanish are particularly proud of the appetizers that precede the meal, and the lady of the house should be complimented.

The style of eating is consistent with the rest of Europe. Forks are placed in the left hand and food is scooped on the back side of the fork. Popular sandwiches such as hamburgers are eaten with a knife and fork. When fruit such as an orange or apple is served as dessert, a knife and fork will accompany the fruit. Hands should not be used to peel the orange or apple.

The extended family plays an integral role in Spanish society. Elderly parents and grandparents are encouraged to live at home. Parents play a key role in finding proper jobs for their children, and sometimes friends will help secure positions for another friend's children.

Business dress is generally very formal. Spaniards will always try to look their best – even the porters will be dressed in suits and ties. Uniforms for the workers are very popular in industry: street cleaners, rubbish collectors, carpenters and others will wear distinctive one-piece uniforms.

Spanish businessmen view the 'power tie' (bright red or yellow) as absolutely tasteless. Dark suits with navy or grey ties are preferred.

Castilian Spanish, considered the purest form of Spanish, is spoken by about 75 per cent of the population. Catalan, a separate language, is spoken by 15 per cent of the population, mostly in the Barcelona region. Basque is spoken by 2 per cent. English is not widely spoken, but interpreters are readily available in larger cities.

Spaniards are very expressive speakers and converse rapidly, using many hand gestures. Their hands are never concealed in their pockets. When meeting a Spaniard for the first time, a foreigner will find himself interrupted frequently – but the reverse is considered offensive. Spaniards can be very frank when it comes to cultural blunders by foreigners and they don't hesitate to point out the errors; a thick skin may be needed in the early stages of learning to work with Spaniards.

Catholicism is embraced by 98 per cent of the population. Until 1966 it was the state religion, and it was against the law to hold non-Catholic church services. Protestant and Jewish services were held only in foreign embassies. There is still considerable job discrimination between Catholics and non-Catholics.

Business cards are essential in business and social situations. It is not uncommon to find that the porter in your apartment or housing block will hand his calling card to you. Calling cards reflect the Spanish emphasis on social decorum.

Negotiations with Spanish business people should be handled with extreme patience. Negotiations often begin over lunch or dinner, generally festive gatherings, with alcohol served throughout the meal. It is wise to accept the 'national' brandy, Jerez, before beginning the meal. Red wine will subsequently follow throughout the meal.

The one stereotype that still holds true in Spanish society is the concept of *mañana* – tomorrow. In negotiations, if there are issues that need immediate action, they must be communicated forcefully (but cordially) to the Spanish counterpart. If a foreigner is always demanding that every issue be resolved immediately, the Spanish tend to view the demands as not important.

Family names and titles are used to address people until one becomes better acquainted. Only then can first names be used, in both business and social relations.

Spanish traditional courtesy and hospitality apply to business relations. If invited to a home, take flowers for the wife or almost any kind of gift except food. Business visitors should be prepared to reciprocate in a restaurant.

## HISTORY AND GOVERNMENT

The mainland of Spain covers about five-sixths of the Iberian Peninsula. The country also includes the Canary Islands, the Balearic Islands, and the North African enclaves of Ceuta and Melilla. Madrid is the geographical, political, and cultural centre of the nation.

There are six distinct regions in Spain. Castile, in the centre of the country encompasses Madrid, and is the most densely populated. Castilian is spoken there. Catalonia is in the eastern part of the country and includes Barcelona. The Catalans are called the 'Europeans' of Spain and are known for their aggressiveness in business. Picasso spent his boyhood there.

A mountainous terrain has made it difficult for Spain's people to mingle easily. Regions are separated from each other by nature, and all of Spain tends to be insulated from the rest of Europe by the Pyrenees. Tradition has been able to survive in this country because of the difficulty of movement across its uneven terrain, which has done a good job of deterring outside forces from penetrating the peninsula.

Despite the country's ill-starred past as a target for occupying forces, it has emerged in post-war times as a remarkably stable and resilient nation, fully committed to the vision of a united Europe. A parliamentary monarchy, the system allows a strong monarch and a strong prime minister to coexist. The Cortes (legislature) consists of 350 members, and the senate of 257.

## ECONOMY

Since the 1950s Spain has begun to take a major role in world business. In 1955 it became a member of the United Nations, the International Monetary Fund, and the World Bank. In 1958 it joined the Organization for Economic Cooperation and Development. In 1959, with gold and foreign exchange reserves almost exhausted, Spain was forced to turn to international agencies and foreign governments for financial help and advice.

A turning point for the economy came in 1959. The Stabilization Plan carried out much needed fiscal and commercial reform and put Spain's finances in order. One of the first aims of the government in 1959 was to encourage a variety of new industries, thus allowing Spain to be less dependent on imports. The controlling head of this drive was located in the National Institute of Industry (INI), a state holding company.

Among its many ambitious projects was the production of petro-chemicals, fuel, fertilizers, refineries, and iron and steel plants. Other enterprises were power generation, textiles, automobile manufacturing, mining, communications, aeronautics, and machinery. INI's greatest success story was the elevation of Spain's shipbuilding industry to the number three rank in the world. Spain is also Europe's largest producer of marine diesel engines.

With the arrival of more liberal policies, foreign investors poured money into such activities as textiles, construction, chemicals, and automobiles. Major foreign investors are the United States, Germany and Switzerland. Spain's net tourist revenues are the highest in the world.

The country has a free market economy with less governmental ownership of principal industries than in most modern industrial societies. Spain is attempting to expand its industrial base by importing certain modern technologies and subsequently expanding exports of manufactured goods.

The Spanish GDP has grown at a very healthy rate and is expected to continue growing. The healthy economic growth can be associated with strong export growth. But unemployment continues to plague the Spanish economy; the rate hovers around 20 per cent (double the OECD average).

The labour force has continued to grow rapidly, due in part to the increased level of women in the work force.

## BIBLIOGRAPHY

Kompass Espana, SA, *Kompass Espana*. New York: IPC Business Press, Ltd, Annual.

Lieberman, Sima, *The Contemporary Spanish Economy: A Historical Perspective*. London and Boston: Allen and Unwin, 1982.

Lopez-Claros, Augusto, *The Search for Efficiency in the Adjustment Process: Spain in the 1980s*. Washington, DC: International Monetary Fund, 1988.

OECD, *Spain*. Paris: Organization for Economic Cooperation and Development, Annual.

Preston, Paul, *The Triumph of Democracy in Spain*. London; New York: Methuen, 1986.

Tamemes, Ramon, *Introduccion a la Economia Espanola*. Madrid: Alianza, 1985.

# 18  Sweden

## EUROPE'S BLUE-EYED 'JAPANESE'

Several years ago, the national 'personalities' of Norway, Sweden and Denmark were categorized in a study at Scandinavian Airlines Systems, the carrier jointly owned by the three governments. The study showed that the adventurous Norwegians made up the largest proportion of pilots, the outgoing Danes held the most sales and marketing jobs, and the Swedes dominated engineering and technical posts.

Swedes have a well-earned reputation as the most down-to-earth of the three, as problem-solvers and sticklers for detail and accuracy. Throughout their history, Swedes have demonstrated an ability to find 'reasonable' solutions to controversial issues, a willingness to negotiate their way to a goal. These strengths show up in their people today.

Clues to the origin of the Swedish character must be sought in the country's history. For 150 years, Sweden has been neutral – a stance that remains central to the nation, despite new critics who warn that the very idea is outdated. Swedes tend to stand back and watch with a sense of superiority as other nations quarrel with each other. Analytical to a fault, they take more pleasure in the role of arbiter than participant.

In business, however, they show considerable individual competitive zeal. Similar to the Japanese, they reserve their best competitive weapons for their foreign rivals. The power of Swedish multinationals such as Electrolux, L.M. Ericsson and SKF attest to the success of the strategy.

As in Japan, a great force in Sweden is the taste for teamwork. In the past few decades, Swedish management has led its European rivals in creating and adopting motivation techniques for workers. In parallel with the country's egalitarian views, Swedish executives like to experiment with new forms of employee-oriented work systems. Only Japan equals Sweden in striving to rethink the world of work.

Yet with all this enlightenment, about fifteen families control one-third of the industrial base of the country. Through a network of banks, investment houses, and cross-ownership of shares, the captains of industry thus can dictate the pace of the economy. Sweden's hierarchy as a result tends towards nepotism, and having connections with the big families is a major asset. Foreign executives new to the culture complain that Swedes can be cliquish and exclude outsiders.

Sweden is a distinctly secular society. Although some 93 per cent of Swedes are nominally Evangelical Lutherans, church attendance is low, and the church's impact on Swedish political and cultural life is minimal.

In his book *Sweden: The Prototype of Modern Society*, Richard Thomassin lists some of the traits that help explain the Swedes:

- Legalism – Swedes invariably do things strictly according to the rules. In Stockholm, for example, one can always spot the foreigners. They are the ones who cross the street against a red traffic light.
- Privacy – more so than in other countries, Swedes draw sharp distinctions between a person's public role and private life. Visitors, even friends, do not just 'drop in'.
- Proper behaviour – displays of open emotion are rare. Good manners and a sense of decorum are nearly always observed.
- Aesthetics – Swedes show a meticulous concern for design in every-thing from office and household furniture to cars, trucks, boats and buildings.

Doing business in Sweden requires the typical restraints of northern European culture. Good planning, tidiness, neatness and thoroughness are valued concepts. It is wise to confirm appointments by letter, telex or telephone, and to arrive punctually for appointments. Handshaking with a firm grip is a standard practice; eyes should meet. A foreign visitor normally presents a business card and a modest gift.

Swedes are formidable negotiators. Most managers have had technical training and are skilful with facts and numbers. A frequent complaint of Swedish business people is that foreign business execu-tives are often inadequately prepared. Careful preparation, ensuring that all facts and ramifications have been covered, are hallmarks of Swedish business.

Little time is wasted between the exchange of initial pleasantries and the start of business discussions. During negotiations, the foreign visitor should be somewhat formal in manner. Negotiations tend to move at a quick, businesslike pace.

The Swedes sometimes have an aversion to conflict, and as a result may avoid discussing areas of potential difficulty. A skilful negotiator will gently redirect questions to areas where the differences have not been resolved. 'Yes' means 'yes', but 'no' often means they are willing to continue negotiating. When an agreement has been reached, this will be indicated orally, and a Swedish business person's word is good. Agreements are confirmed by a handshake, then in writing.

Entertaining plays a large role in relations with foreigners. Normally invitations are for dinner parties at the host's private home. Manners and traditions at the dining table can be complex. Guests are placed in order of rank, even in private homes. Therefore a person with a doctoral degree sits nearer the hostess than a person with a bachelor's degree.

During the dinner, foreigners are sometimes initiated into the Nordic *Skal* (pronounced *Skol*) ritual – Swedes enjoy explaining it. At any time after the host's toast of welcome to all guests, you may catch somebody's eye – start with the lady on your right – raise your glass, nod slightly, say *Skal*, then drink. Catch another person's eye again, nod slightly, put your glass down; at the end of the meal, if you are guest of honour, offer a general *Skal* of thanks to host and hostess.

In conversation, most anything goes. Neutrality is a sensitive but much debated topic. Religion can be talked about freely. Remember that the average Swede is well-educated and will enjoy an intelligent argument. There are few taboos, but Swedes are tired of hearing the foreign clichés about sex, suicides and drunkenness in their land.

Ceremonious manners account for part of Sweden's charm. At a business dinner, formality will prevail. Here are a few tips:

- Flowers or chocolates must be brought for the hostess when invited to the home for dinner.
- Never stand with your hands in your pockets.
- A man should always walk on the left side of the lady.
- Toasts are made with the utmost decorum. Your host first proposes the toast, and then you are free to toast the woman sitting on your left. Lift your glass stiffly and look into her eyes.
- Conversation is frequently carried on in the third person. This tends to make the person you are talking to a fictional character.
- Swedes are greatly affected by their climate. They talk about it even more than the English.
- When offering a light for a cigarette, some Swedes show the extreme courtesy of taking the match and offering it back to you, still lit, before lighting their own cigarette.
- Thank the hostess before leaving the table.
- Write or at least telephone the following day to thank the hostess for the evening spent at her home. If you later run into your host or hostess by chance, repeat the thanks.

Greetings play an integral role in this country bound up in formalities. Hats are always lifted for friends, acquaintances, and even people you meet for the first time. It is not uncommon to see a younger girl curtsy or to observe a young boy bowing to an elder.

The long, liquid lunch is out, as Swedish executives are generally averse to mixing business with too much pleasure. Meeting for an early evening drink is becoming more common, however.

Swedish business dress tends to be slightly more conservative and formal than styles in many Western countries. A dark business suit is generally acceptable for any business occasion, except when a dinner jacket or formal wear may be required. Among younger people, the stress on formal attire is not as prevalent. However, Swedes are generally quite conscious of their appearance.

## HISTORY AND GOVERNMENT

The Vikings, their expeditions, culture and myths lend a special richness to the history of Sweden. The Swedish Viking chief Rurik is said to have founded Russia, and wars with Nordic neighbours raged for centuries. But quiet descended on Sweden after a revolt and coup in 1809, sparked by heavy losses in one of the ill-fated wars. Gustaf IV Adolf was deposed, and Juan Bernadotte, an acclaimed and able commander under Napoleon, acceded to the throne. His accession brought with it the Instrument of Government, a document that began to lay down constitutional powers for the king, government and parliament, and thus Sweden's move towards democracy.

Sweden today is a constitutional monarchy with a parliamentary government. Carl XVI Gustaf has been the ruling King since 1973. The Parliament consists of one chamber whose members are directly elected for simultaneous three-year terms.

Sweden is the largest and by far the most populous of the Scandinavian countries. It covers the southern and eastern coasts of the peninsula and includes the two largest Baltic islands of Gotland and Olad. Sweden is a long, narrow country with an area of 174,000 square miles, the fourth largest in Europe. It is a land of immense forests broken up by some 96,000 lakes. Rivers have been harnessed to provide hydroelectric power.

With a population of 8.3 million people, the Swedes have ample space – an average of 47 people per square mile as compared to 500 in England or 55 in the United States. Life is centred around the family, and although most families are town-dwellers, they still have a great love and enthusiasm for the outdoors. Life-expectancy of the Swede is the highest in the world – 75 years for men and 79 for women, and infant mortality is the lowest in the world.

Like other Scandinavian peoples, the Swedes are one of the least mixed of all European cultures. The stereotype fits: men and women of tall stature, blue-eyed and flaxen-haired. This has changed only slightly in the past few decades due to immigration from Eastern Europe. The only distinct racial minority are the 10,000 Lapps, or *Samer* as they call themselves, in Swedish Lapland. About 2,000 of them are still living a nomadic life.

## ECONOMY

A relatively small home market has induced many Swedish companies to be export-oriented, with often 75 per cent of revenues coming from overseas. In recent years, larger companies have had notable success in carrying out aggressive overseas expansion. Swedish executives, as a result, tend to be far more worldly than their counterparts in other countries. Often they speak two or three foreign languages fluently, and move comfortably in other cultures.

At home, a strong advantage to the manufacturing industries has traditionally been low-cost hydroelectric power, now providing 27 per cent of the country's energy and 56 per cent of its electricity. But the success with which these resources and others are converted into industrial products for sales at home and abroad can be attributed to two other factors: the Swedish drive for increasing productivity and high standards in quality.

The three most important categories of state expenditures are national defence, education and social welfare. Social welfare benefits account for the largest share, 25 per cent. National defence, although Sweden pursues a policy of nonalignment, makes up about 8 per cent of the budget. Education accounts for 13 per cent of expenditures for such things as technical research and new educational facilities.

In several areas, the government shows a much more friendly attitude towards business than in most socialist countries. First, the corporate tax regime is regarded as the most liberal in the world. Second, depreciation laws are also very liberal. Another good example is the rule on inventory reserves, which allows inventories to be carried on books at anywhere from 40 per cent to 100 per cent of value, at the option of the company.

The regulation of business practices, though effective, often has an almost casual character. Whenever possible, formal controls are avoided, even in the area of anti-trust. Legislation can be intentionally vague, with emphasis on discussion rather than coercion.

Much of the harmony in the government–business relationship can be attributed to their close agreement on the goals of the economy. Both accept that industry needs capital for expansion and that consumer spending must be held down to do this, usually by raising taxes.

Industrialization came late to Sweden. The twentieth century has been a period of growing prosperity that continued through the 1950s when Sweden came to be viewed as a near-ideal state achieving social security, equality, and economic prosperity while remaining a liberal democracy.

Although the people are industrious, a prime factor in Sweden's prosperity is the abundance of natural resources. Its forests supply the greatest amount of paper pulp in the world, and high-grade iron ore is turned into the high-quality steel needed for such diverse products as roller bearings, razor blades and Swedish cars, trucks and buses.

Yet in many ways the system does not seem to be working as efficiently as it has in the past. Many fear that Swedes will not be able to maintain their standard of living as the global economy grows more ruthlessly competitive.

## BIBLIOGRAPHY

Hamilton, Carl B, *A Swedish View of 1992*. London: Royal Institute of International Affairs, 1989.

MacDonald, Greg, *The Nordic Countries and Mulinational Enterprises: Employment Effects and Foreign Direct Investment*. Geneva: International Labour Office, 1989.

Milner, Henry, *Sweden: Social Democracy in Practice*. New York: Oxford University Press, 1989.

Phillips-Martinsson, Jean, *Swedes as Others See Them*. Stockholm: Affarsforlaget, 1981.

Ross, John F.L., *Neutrality and International Sanctions: Sweden, Switzerland and Collective Security*. New York: Praeger, 1989.

Skandinaniski Enskilda Banken, *Some Data About Sweden 1985-1986*, Stockholm, 1985.

Swedish Institute, *The Swedish Economy*. Stockholm, February 1986.

Tomasson, Richard F., *Sweden: Prototype of Modern Society*. New York: Random House, 1970.

Wadensjoo, Costa, *Sweden Liberhermods*, 1979.

# 19   Switzerland

## LESS THAN SPLENDID ISOLATION

There is a saying in Switzerland that a person who is late either doesn't have a Swiss watch or didn't use a Swiss train. As in the case of most amusing aphorisms, a grain of truth lurks behind the laughter. The Swiss start from the rather smug assumption that their isle of tranquillity is a place of superior government, economy and social structure. Indeed, the trains do run on time and the watches work, but the country's determined arm's-length distance from its neighbours may be difficult to sustain in a more integrated post-1992 Europe and a more interdependent world economy. The Swiss are understandably accustomed to being successful, but their splendid isolation is not the safe haven from life's turmoil it once was.

The early steps towards integration of the twelve economies of the European Community (EC) are already causing discrimination against Swiss citizens resident in other European countries, especially in the lack of recognition of Swiss professional qualifications. In addition, the gradual rationalization of industry among the EC member states is likely to exclude Swiss companies as the EC begins to build businesses with the critical mass for global competition.

The key Swiss economic advantage in recent decades has been banking secrecy – the ability to attract funds from throughout the world and shelter them from the client's tax authorities. As moral pressure to bring Swiss banks into line with the world standard is mounting, some forward-thinking Swiss fear that a decline in the fortunes of the country's financial institutions would be catastrophic to the national economy. 'When banking secrecy goes, we become a Third World country', one worried banker said recently.

Transformation to an economy more like that of its neighbours would be no easy task. The Alps cover about 60 per cent of the country's land surface, and the Jura an additional 10 per cent. One-fourth of Switzerland's area is uninhabitable, as it consists of lakes, glaciers, and high mountains. The challenge of the 1990s will be to integrate with foreign partners without losing the Swiss devotion to quality and efficiency.

Doing business in Switzerland, however, can be a brisk and rewarding experience. The traditions of quality, efficiency and proper behaviour apply to dealings with each other as well as with foreign partners. Strict rules of formality hold sway, and in meetings with foreign colleagues, little time is spent on chitchat or personal matters. The Swiss want, above all, to be efficient in business. People are taught from a young age to work hard and to appreciate a job well done. Wasteful business relations, like poor workmanship, tend to be considered disgraceful.

A Swiss company is likely to be run and organized in a formal way. The hierarchy in the company plays an important role, and respect is shown to top executives in the company. During a meeting, business etiquette demands that particular attention be paid to addressing important matters to top management. Rise when someone new enters the room.

Loud speech and boisterous laughter are not considered in good taste. The atmosphere can sometimes turn informal and more casual, but the visitor should not take the initiative in easing the tone. Improper posture or sloppy attire categorize one as ill-mannered and ill-bred.

A lifetime of following rules makes the Swiss resistant to sudden change. A visitor should therefore be careful not to suggest major modifications in the course of a strategy or plan, even if he feels that a decision could be obtained more easily by doing so. The key is to adapt to the Swiss company's ways.

Meetings are conducted in logical order, moving to new topics only when an answer has been found to the preceding question. Swiss executives usually get to the point without delay they do not introduce subjects irrelevant to the purpose of the meeting.

It is not rare for a meeting to be conducted over a meal in a restaurant. This traditionally male-dominated country (women have only been granted the to right to vote since 1971) does not expect a husband to bring his wife to dinner unless specifically invited to do so.

As in Germanic Europe, it is best to reconfirm appointments, even though once made appointments will be kept. It is important to arrive at the appointed hour. First names are not commonly used between new acquaintances, and excessive touching during conversation is not customary. Proper posture is considered to be part of the well-bred individual. The Swiss are a formal people.

The handshake is the standard form of greeting. A person should shake hands with any man or woman he is introduced to, waiting for the woman to offer her hand first.

Personal life and family life are private matters. Your Swiss colleagues will volunteer such information if they wish to, and only at that point should you feel safe in showing an interest.

Swiss people dislike self-promotion or public display of one's accomplishments. It is preferable to avoid speaking about oneself too much, as it may be considered boasting. Talking politics is acceptable but one should be careful not to show extreme opinions.

Culture is highly regarded, and most people are knowledgeable about leading artists and their works. The Swiss are great nature-lovers who appreciate and cherish the beauty of the land. They feel flattered when visitors show an interest in or admiration for it.

When invited to a private home, a small impersonal gift for the hostess, candy or flowers, is welcome. Perfume is generally considered too personal. When buying flowers, one should remember that flowers given as gifts have a special and eloquent meaning. For example, red flowers mean 'I love you' in Switzerland, and although this is tending to disappear as a literal message, it is wise to ask advice from the florist.

Guests should shake hands with every family member, starting with the hostesss, both when arriving and when departing. The host will indicate when and where to sit. Guests should always wait for the hostess to sit down first, and never begin eating before she does. Everything on the plate should be eaten, and the best compliment is to take second helpings. In Swiss restaurants, meals tend to be served in two helpings. Save room.

Most professional people in Switzerland are multilingual but one should not be overconfident that one's language is being perfectly understood. It is best to speak slowly and to avoid slang expressions. If you have any knowledge of your host's native language, do not hesitate to try it.

Some useful etiquette tips:

- Direct eye contact is the norm.
- When departing the home of a friend after dinner, it is polite to shake hands with all members of the family.
- Clothing tends to be formal and conservative. Loud styles are frowned upon. A man should wear a suit and tie when going to a meeting, to a restaurant, or when invited to dinner at a private home.
- For women, clothing is likely to be more conservative as well, and extremely informal clothing such as slacks and shorts are almost never considered proper except for resort wear.
- It is considered bad manners to be sitting sloppily, or to stretch one's legs out. A relaxed but composed posture is recommended.
- It is considered rude or impolite to rest one's elbows on the table or to support one's head with a hand while having their elbow on the table.

## HISTORY AND GOVERNMENT

Population numbers about 6.5 million and is a mixture of European stock. Originally inhabited by the Helvetic Celts, Switzerland was conquered by Julius Caesar, then invaded by German tribes after the decline of the

Roman Empire. Many cultures have influenced Switzerland, making ethnic groups difficult to define.

The country has no natural exploitable resources, and lacks a coastline and a common language, yet it is an international financial power, and is considered a model of economic stability for its neighbours. Its citizens enjoy one of the highest standards of living in the world, and in many ways a most enviable quality of life.

Situated in the centre of Europe, it is bounded by Germany, Austria, Liechtenstein, Italy, and France. It is one of the few countries that has no direct access to the sea. The large cities and industrial sections of Switzerland are concentrated in the lowlands, between the two mountain ranges.

The capital city is Berne, with a population of about 150,000. Other main cities are Zurich (354,500), Basel (176,200), Geneva (159,500) and Lausanne (126,200). These constitute the key business regions.

Switzerland is a democratic confederation divided into twenty cantons and six half-cantons. Its official name is the Swiss Confederation. It is a federal state, governed by a parliament with two chambers, the National Council and the Council of States. The National Council has 200 members, proportionately distributed. The Council of States is made up of two representatives from each of the twenty full cantons and one from each of the six half-cantons. The executive council, which represents the executive branch, comprises seven members. The four major political parties are the Radical Democrats, the Social Democrats, the Christian Democrats, and Volkspartei (Peasants' Party).

The country has a long tradition of neutrality. It has not sent troops into foreign wars since 1514. In 1815, the Confederation declared Switzerland's 'perpetual' neutrality.

About 50 per cent of the population are Roman Catholic, and 48 per cent Protestant. Romantsch is the least common of the four official languages, and is mostly spoken in the southeast section of the country. German is spoken by most people in the south, middle, and north-central parts of Switzerland. French is spoken in the western portion of the country.

## ECONOMY

The Swiss economy has a long history of strong performance. It is expected to continue to grow, although at slower rates, into the 1990s. The primary goal of Swiss fiscal and monetary authorities is to hold down inflation. The fear is that either an overheated economy or sharp increases in imported fuel costs will rekindle inflation. As of 1985, Switzerland imported 66 per cent of its energy needs, and this figure is expected to remain above 50 per cent for the near future. Over the long term, however, the Swiss plan to increase their use of gas and electricity, thereby reducing their dependence on foreign oil.

The Swiss have traditionally maintained a low unemployment rate, and in fact have required a large number of foreign workers. In 1984, foreign workers represented 22 per cent of the workforce.

Labour is highly skilled, and the government together with private enterprise, makes an effort to maintain this high level. Employer-employee relations are famous for their record of peaceful collaboration. They are governed by collective agreement, which is observed by all parties. Workers are rather bourgeois, like everyone else, and want to live well. The relationships between workers, employers and unions are based on mutual esteem, discussions between parties are continuous and open, and only in extreme cases are differences settled by arbitration.

There is a strong union movement in Switzerland, but membership is voluntary. With a continuing recession it is possible that unions would become more militant, but there have been no organized strikes of importance in the past forty years.

Although profit-sharing requirements are not compulsory, some larger enterprises have introduced schemes to allocate additional remuneration on the basis of profitability. Unions and individuals are as a whole more interested in high remuneration than in the nationality of investors and management. Therefore, except for the left-wing, which denounces 'imperialism' (mainly of the US), the attitude of labour is more or less one of indifference.

Collective agreements lay down certain minimum levels of wages that are only applicable to beginners with no experience in the occupation. Otherwise, wages and salaries are usually based on private agreement. The regular working week is 46 hours in factories and 40 to 44 hours in offices. The minimum vacation period is two weeks per year, but some cantons have increased it to three weeks.

Switzerland's main trading partner is Germany. About 20 per cent of Swiss exports go there. The United States absorbs 10 per cent, and European Community countries take about 50 per cent of Swiss exports.

## BIBLIOGRAPHY

Egli, Emil, *Switzerland: A Survey of its Land and People*. Berne: P. Haupt, 1978.

Kung, Emil, *The Secret of Switzerland's Economic Success*. Washington DC: American Enterprise Institute for Public Policy Research, 1978.

Kung, Emil, *Switzerland Economic Survey*. Zurich: Union Bank of Switzerland, Annual.

Luch, Murray J. and Burchhardt, Lukas F. (eds), *Modern Switzerland*. Palo Alto, California: Society for the Promotion of Science and Scholarship, 1978.

Luch, Murray J., *A History of Switzerland: The First 100,000 Years: Before the Beginnings to the Days of the Present*. Palo Alto, California: Society for the Promotion of Science and Scholarship, 1985.

McPhee, John A., *La Place de la Concorde Suisse*. New York: Farrar, Straus, Giroux, 1984.

OECD, *Switzerland*. Paris: Organization for Economic Cooperation and Development, Annual.

Ross, John F.L., *Neutrality and International Sanctions: Sweden, Switzerland and Collective Security*. New York: Praeger, 1989.